# Spain at the Dawn of History

Richard J. Harrison

# Spain at the Dawn of History

Iberians,
Phoenicians
and Greeks

WITH 113 ILLUSTRATIONS

**THAMES AND HUDSON**

*Ancient Peoples and Places*
FOUNDING EDITOR: GLYN DANIEL

Title page:   The "Dama de Elche" from Elche (Alicante), is a
masterpiece of Iberian stone carving. Only the upper part
survives, but this was once part of an enthroned statue like
the "Dama de Baza," and dates from between 400 and 350 BC.

First published in the United States in 1988 by
Thames and Hudson Inc., 500 Fifth Avenue,
New York, New York 10110
Library of Congress Catalog Card Number 87-51688

Printed and bound in the German Democratic Republic

# Contents

PART II

# Preface

MY FIRST CONTACT with the ancient Iberians, who lived in what today we call Spain and Portugal, came through reading the book which Professor Antonio Arribas wrote in this same series for Thames and Hudson in 1963, and which was used in my under-graduate courses in archaeology at Cambridge University. In the Tripos which we studied in those days Iberians didn't figure prominently, and when they did put in an appearance, it was usually accompanied by the lament that we couldn't say much about them for the lack of modern accounts, or reliable excavations. So they got short shrift, which was a pity.

Beginning in the mid-1960s, Spain transformed her archaeology as profoundly as her economy, and much of the lead was given by the late Professor Martín Almagro Basch in his twin roles as Director of the National Museum in Madrid, and head of the Subdirección General de Arqueología which gave permits and money to excavate. The result was like moving from twilight into bright sunshine. Inevitably, the flood of discoveries took time to describe correctly, and the first assimilations of this rich harvest were, rightly, made by historians who had established models into which they could place the new finds. It seemed rather simple and logical at the time, and was undoubtedly easier than making original ones to accommodate the new discoveries. I think the time has come to change focus a little and to try a different type of account which doesn't begin from such straight historical conceptions. I see this period through the eyes of a prehistorian, but one with the training of a field archaeologist, which is why this book takes its present form. It is built around themes such as writing and mining, and is united by the orientalizing phenomenon, rather than structured by a table of historical events. Of course, some historical documentation is of immense value, especially for the oldest periods, and I use it where appropriate: thank goodness we have it!

Selecting themes has been the hardest task of all and lack of space forced me to leave out a detailed account of the Iberian world under Roman influence, a period known as the 'Baja Epoca'. I saw my task first and foremost to portray accurately the substance of recent discoveries, even though some were roughly excavated like Cancho Roano, or remain largely unpublished like the cities of Ategua or Ullastret. I chose to centre attention upon what is now known certainly, and discuss important issues where real progress is being made, like our understanding of ancient urbanism, or the role ideology played in the artistic works that suddenly appear after 500 BC. There is a great success story here, due to archaeologists' fieldwork in Spain, and to a far lesser degree in Portugal, which merits wider recognition. This is a small part of it.

In citing dates I have followed the convention that has been established for many years in the journal *Antiquity*; dates based on radiocarbon years are cited as 'bc', while dates which belong to the solar or historical calendars are cited as 'BC'. In fact, radiocarbon dates are only used in Chapter 2, and they are not calibrated.

Finally, I am happy to thank many friends who have helped me at one time or another. I especially value the advice of Dr Manuel Bendalá Galán of the Universidad Autonoma, Madrid; Professor Guillermo Fatás Cabeza and Dr Francisco Marco Simón of the Universidad de Zaragoza; Dr Paul Craddock of the British Museum Research Laboratory, Professor Beno Rothenberg of the University of London, and Dr Christopher Gerrard of the University of Bristol.

*Saragossa 1987*

# Introduction

THE DEVELOPMENT of Iberian culture and society between 1000 and 200 BC is the theme of this book. It is an account told almost entirely from records that have been dug from the ground, written from things we can see, touch and hold today, so that we can believe what our own senses detect. It is an archaeological account that makes no pretence to be historical, but which develops subjects which archaeology is uniquely well suited to handle. The central task is to explain the rise of a new cultural expression in art, script and the most fascinating of all, society that we call Iberian.

It is a study in two parts. The first shows what Bronze Age societies were like when ships from Phoenicia reached their shores; then how the colonies were set up, and the revolutionary changes got under-way in the seventh century. This could be called the colonial experience in Iberia. It was repeated in the sixth and fifth centuries by the Carthaginians in the Balearic Islands, and by the Massiliote Greeks (i.e. Greeks resident in what would be modern Marseilles) in Catalonia in the sixth century. The second part describes significant achievements of the orientalizing period one at a time, showing how they began and grew. This is the material expression of Iberian culture.

## The colonists' homelands

For an understanding of the colonial experience we must turn to the eastern Mediterranean and the homelands of the Phoenicians and Greeks (*ill. 1*). The lands the Phoenicians inhabited lay on the coasts stretching from the modern state of Syria, down to Lebanon, and into northern Israel, and are characterized more by their fragmented terrain and accessibility from the sea than by their fertility or mineral wealth. The small city-states that flourished on this coast were constantly in contact with Egypt to the south, and the Mesopotamian civilizations to the east, often acting as intermediaries between the greater powers. On some occasions they were directly subjugated by them and paid tribute, on others they were free, or at least had a precarious independence. The Phoenician city-states were already ancient kingdoms in the second millennium BC, but their history takes on a special interest for us after 1100 BC.

Following a period of Egyptian rule, the small states of Syria and Palestine reasserted their independence after 1025 BC, and were able to

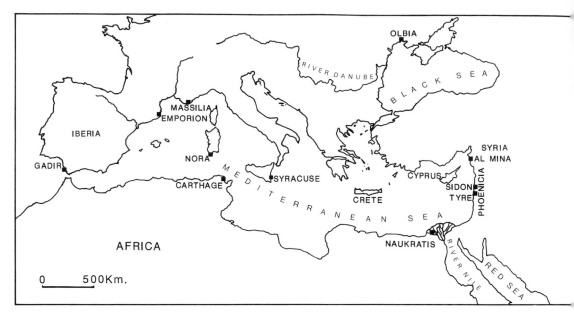

1 A map of the Mediterranean Sea locating some of the important Phoenician and Greek sites mentioned in the text.

keep it for a century and a half; it was the time when the Old Testament kings David and Solomon ruled in Israel, and King Hiram in Tyre. The leading states were Sidon and Tyre, followed by lesser ones in Byblos, Beirut and Aradus. The first two pursued a policy of expansive overseas trade from 1100 BC which led them ever further afield, first to Cyprus, then to Crete, the rest of the Aegean, and by the tenth or even eleventh century to Sardinia in the central Mediterranean. These advances were stimulated by the need to find fresh supplies of raw materials to feed the growing industries which manufactured luxuries back in the homeland. Trade prospered greatly, and Phoenicians supplied both Egypt and Assyria with expensive goods. But during the ninth and eighth centuries Assyrian pressure increased steadily upon these vulnerable little states, forcing them to pay tribute. Then, from being tributary states they were reduced by conquest to become dependencies, beginning with the attacks of the Assyrian king Tiglath Pileser III in the 740s, and ending finally with the fall of Tyre to the Babylonian king Nebuchadnezzar in 573 BC.

It is noticeable that the Phoenician expansion into Sicily, Sardinia and Spain in the eighth century coincides with the loss of their residual independence; the conquest of their mother cities probably forced many Phoenicians to become emigrants and seek a new life in colonies and trading stations out in the west. One feature of this movement must be emphasized; there was never a coordinated effort or scheme which directed their trade and emigration, but rather a myriad of individual decisions, with each independent state acting as it saw fit.

Greece at this time was emerging from her Dark Age, the impoverished period between the collapse of the Mycenaean world in 1200 BC and the reappearance of new political forms based on independent city-states after 800 BC. From the ninth century onwards, contacts with Cyprus and the Phoenician coasts had quickened Greek interest in the Near East, renewing direct contacts that had been broken for two or three centuries. The two fundamental phenomena that stand out from this time are the rise of the *polis* in the Archaic period, with its first tentative steps towards urban life and public buildings, and the great colonizing surges that were to take Greeks from Gibraltar to the Caucasus by 650 BC.

Within the Greek colonial episode we can distinguish those establishments which were entirely of a mercantile nature – such as the ones in the town of Al Mina on the Syrian coast near the Orontes river, with a Greek presence by 800 BC, or at the island of Ischia off the Bay of Naples in southern Italy from 775 BC – and true colonies formed by emigrants from Greece. These latter were set up from the beginning as *poleis*, or city-states in their own right, and usually sought out locations with good harbours and fertile soils close by; Syracuse is one example. The heyday of the colonizing enterprises was between 750 and 650 BC, although important foundations were still made in the following century; true markets like Emporion (northeast Spain) and Naukratis (in the Nile delta of Egypt) belong to this later surge, set up after 600 BC. Why Greeks should emigrate in such numbers is the subject of much debate, but it is apparent that strong social pressures in some city-states lay behind their colonial foundations; land hunger, poverty, political dissent and overpopulation all played a role. As with the Phoenician colonization in the eighth century, there was no overall movement or policy followed by the Greeks in their spread outwards from the Aegean.

The story in Iberia goes back to the turn of the first millennium BC, when human groups everywhere lived with a Bronze Age technology and flint tools for farming. Contact with them was made by the Phoenicians from Syria and Lebanon who established colonies just after 800 BC on the south coast. In the space of less than a century, they stimulated the native societies to emulate eastern models to the point where they were transformed utterly. This is the watershed of the seventh century BC, the episode that we call orientalizing. It was a cultural process of remarkable intensity which changed Greek and Etruscan societies to their roots at the same time, and had no less effect in Iberia. From this crucible of seventh-century innovation were cast the forms that were to stamp Iberian culture with its Mediterranean individuality. No longer a small-scale, tribal society of farmers with a basic technology, but one able to build towns on the eastern pattern, raise foodstuffs to feed their inhabitants, work iron, mine silver, and exploit art for ideological ends. The secrets of writing too were mastered, and scripts devised for Iberian languages. From the sixth to the third centuries indigenous societies thrived, but their creation lies in the orientalizing experience.

## The Iberians' achievement

The uniform exterior of Iberian culture hides a political and social mosaic underneath. Iberians lacked political and linguistic unity yet shared an undeniable affinity which set them apart from their neighbours in the interior. By the time Classical soldiers and travellers knew Iberia sufficiently well to write about it sensibly, these groups had multiplied bewilderingly into tribes and peoples and lands, Iberian all. Sorting this documentation out into something usable is not the task of archaeology, nor is it of immediate interest here; what is worth looking at is the fact that the same pattern persisted under the Iberian stylistic hegemony as had formed it in the later Bronze Age. It is simply recounted in more luxurious detail for later periods. The causes behind it are probably the same: a growing population unevenly spread, and not necessarily with the greatest numbers occupying the most fertile tracts of land; varied political systems, with some areas ruled by chiefs, others with hereditary elites, but all likely to possess only fragile authority from which to exercise their power; and distinct forms of land ownership.

This world came into being in the orientalizing period. It was the product of forces released under the shock of colonial settlements which were stocked by men and women wholly outside the control of the indigenous peoples. The initial effects are seen as the oldest and intensest orientalizing stage enveloped the lower Guadalquivir valley and the regions westwards to Huelva, where a local tradition of kingship had evolved in the Bronze Age. By contrast, the episode in Catalonia took place amid societies that were materially poor and politically underdeveloped. And on the Balearic Islands the orientalizing process began in the late sixth century, organized by the Carthaginians based on Ibiza. Other areas that were later strongly Iberian in their material culture, such as the Levant and the southeast, did not experience this stage, or if they did, the transformation is unidentified.

The product is Iberian material culture, recognizable by 600 to 550 BC in western Andalusia, centred in the Guadalquivir valley. It is clearly the same society that was called Tartessian by the Greeks, and later Bronze Age by modern archaeologists. This is the motor which develops the dominant fashions that take over in pottery, metalwork, forms of jewellery, and probably matters relating to cult and burial customs. It is not a small, fertile nucleus, but a region with many independently powerful individuals within it, probably organized on a territorial basis like city-states. Such power bases arose directly in the orientalizing period, some from people who represented 'old money', ancestral wealth and status inherited from their fathers, and others who had seized opportunities and enriched themselves by their own efforts. The fashions engendered in western Andalusia spread swiftly by exchange and imitation, so that by 550 to 500 BC, similar styles of Iberian pottery with geometric decoration were being made in Catalonia and Andalusia. Over the whole of Mediterranean Spain the Iberian cultural gloss gave an impression of cultural similarity that in one sense was unitary; it was adopted and followed for the same reasons. Yet we know that just below the surface of this veneer lurked real diversity. So it is that we can look at an artistic style, or a process like iron-working, or fine pottery manufacture, and find it a cultural possession of divers polities, all Iberian, but keeping themselves socially distinguishable. Whether or not these indigenous groups can ever provide us with an historical framework in which to study this period is uncertain. This unity, formed around 500 BC, lasted until about 200 BC when the Roman conquest altered its shape permanently. There is a late extension of Iberianism into the Ebro valley and Pyrenean foothills around 375 to 350 BC.

Prosperity was not an unmixed good. Tensions grew to the point where they flared into warfare which systematically destroyed many Iberian villages in the Levant, and spread, less intensely, to sites in the southeast and Catalonia. Even the city of Ullastret was burned down about 400 BC. The date of these events is controversial, given variously as 425–375, or around 350 BC. Often the ravages were so intense that scraps of fine sculpture that had been smashed to bits had to be reused as common building materials by people attempting to reoccupy their homes; this happened at Elche (Alicante), which had flourished until then. The richest part of the Iberian world escaped, since the turbulence did not disturb western Andalusia. The causes of this violence are not known; internal feuding, raids from the interior, even attacks by the Carthaginians, could all have played a part. Perhaps connected with western Andalusia's security were the systems of small forts that stud the passes and valleys in profusion in Jaén and Cordoba, blocking access from the Meseta.

Despite these violent spasms, the cultural achievement is an impressive one. The Phoenicians and Carthaginians only occupied a narrow strip of land along the south coast, and the Greek colonists had a toehold in the northeast (*ills. 2, 3*). Carthaginian colonization in the Guadalquivir valley as far as Cástulo (near Linares) remains unproven. The rest of the country was unoccupied by colonists, and continued to be governed by indigenous rulers in their own manner. It is they who had chosen deliberately to enter the wider cultural orbit which the colonies represented, and to assimilate the elements they especially admired or which gave advantage over their political rivals. We know little about the individual motives behind the assimilation, but the general ones are likely to have been a desire for enrichment, enlargement, aggrandizement, not just of wealth, but of everything else, too. That is why they take the form

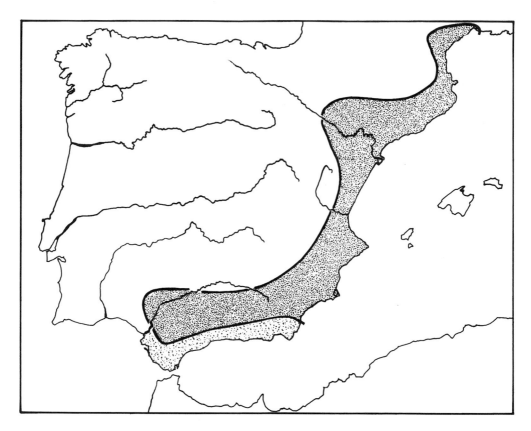

2 Iberian culture at its maximum geographic extent, between 400 and 300 BC. The area of Phoenician and Punic settlement is shown with a lighter texture.

they do: experimenting with cities to form powerful nuclei of little kingdoms; manipulating new styles of iconography to justify authority precariously held; the absorption of alien cults; the enlargement of the agricultural base to feed the new concentrations in the towns and provide commodities to export; and the invention of alphabets suitable for conveying indigenous languages. These changes are all of a sort which benefit a few people enormously, and the rest scarcely at all. That is why they must have been chosen systematically; and that is why the second part of the book follows them as themes.

In each chapter, the innovation is related as directly as possible to its Semitic or Greek original, and its creation, where it is known, within the orientalizing process. This model shows us a new facet of the Iberian achievement: the successful entry into a Mediterranean way of life that was urban, literate, wine-imbibing. Iberian peoples did this in their own style, at their own pace, for over 400 years until they lost their autonomy and were subjugated by Rome.

## Some historical dilemmas

An organization like this depends for its success upon a division that is not arbitrary; it must have authority to work. The authority for this derives from the archaeological testimonies; not just the objects, but also the capacity of the subject to draw legitimate analogies from other disciplines like sociology or geography, and to look at landscapes and exact contexts which so enrich our documentation. It makes a world of difference if colonies have a territory attached to them or not, or if a Phoenician incense burner is found in a Phoenician grave or in a native one. Even if we wanted to write protohistory, it would scarcely be possible from this base, nor is it likely to be done successfully for decades to come. This is because our dates are nowhere more precise than intervals of thirty to fifty years, often much more, because they depend upon the dates when certain types of Greek pottery were made in the Aegean. Once transported long distances, treasured as heirlooms, and used for a generation or two, such pottery loses value as an historical marker; it becomes a different sort of document altogether. Yet, without precise dating one historical claim cannot be tested against another. The escape from this dilemma is to study themes, not Greek or Carthaginian history where Iberia is a sideshow with flickers of interest every now and then. It is these themes that hide real novelties.

In the vanguard is the clear evidence that the Phoenicians were the first to discover the far west. Greek sailors arrived centuries after them and then failed, for whatever reason, to maintain the direct contact they had with southern Spain in the seventh century. Nearly as significantly, we can show that the dominant influence in the orientalizing period, and afterwards, was Semitic; first Phoenician, then Carthaginian. Greek models were important only in Catalonia, in certain classes of artefact, or specific areas of artistic endeavour such as stone sculpture. Older scholarship by ardent Hellenists overvalued the Greek contribution, and those views are fading under the indisputable evidence from excavations. The archaeological record is imperfect, too, and there is no point making empty claims for it. Conscious of this, a rigorous selection of the best excavations and the latest work in the field should help to guide us away from gross error. This ought to make a coherent framework for understanding how the Iberians came to be able to build towns or write their own language, and perhaps the historical sources can help in the future with these matters.

A few comments on historical sources are appropriate. Ancient historians hope, not unreasonably, that archaeology will help them test the validity of their sources by confirming important detail, or by filling in the narratives. Occasionally they find a useful inscription. The weakness in this train of thought lies in the archaeologists' inability to determine exactly *what* historical phenomenon it is that they are observing. General patterns can be found, changes in artefacts shown, and individual events described, without ever giving straight answers to straight historical questions. Thus, the search for the city of Tartessos in the southwest, or the quest to identify the towns and territories attacked by, or allied to, the Barcids when they build the Carthaginian Empire after 237 BC, are unlikely to succeed.

Much rasher are attempts to correlate layers of destruction in Iberian villages with the passage of an army at one date or another. Work of this sort still flourishes in some places, along the lines laid out by the original masters earlier this century, Professor Adolf Schulten and Professor Pedro Bosch Gimpera. Schulten had success with his excavations of Roman military sites; his theories for the earlier periods where textual sources are far fewer were wild, and sank into oblivion. Bosch Gimpera's work on the Iberians has fared better. He excavated in the robust style of the times, and published much, although it was his encyclopaedic synthesis of Iberian history and archaeology that caught public attention. His work is still of great merit and originality. He used the Greek historical accounts as his framework, since they were the only ones to be had, because he came to a subject almost devoid of excavation, with scanty collections of misunderstood artefacts. So he promptly used Classical writers to help him select themes to examine, like the role of Iberian mercenary soldiers in the Sicilian wars, and a chronology to guide his archaeology. One can understand how a philohellenic bias entered into the work done under such restraints. But times change, and in archaeology the factual base enlarges by leaps and bounds, so that today we do not follow the routes charted in the 1930s by Bosch, when even the *idea* of an orientalizing period in Spain was unthinkable!

The story ends with a brief epilogue. It is a sad one, what the Spaniards expressively call the 'Baja Epoca' of Iberian culture, from 200 to 19 BC, the time when Rome intervened decisively in the affairs of the peninsula. These two centuries saw a true impoverishment of Iberian culture, and a study of these events is more properly dealt with as part of the detail of the Roman conquests. The Iberian culture of the 'Baja Epoca' is fundamentally different in that it was a Romanized version of what flourished previously. It was absorbed into a political configuration vastly different from anything known before, and with it new institutions were forged as Rome exploited her new conquest in a radically different manner than had the Carthaginians and Phoenicians.

3 (*Opposite*) The Iberian peninsula together with the major archaeological sites mentioned in Part I.

# PART I

# THE COLONIAL EXPERIENCE

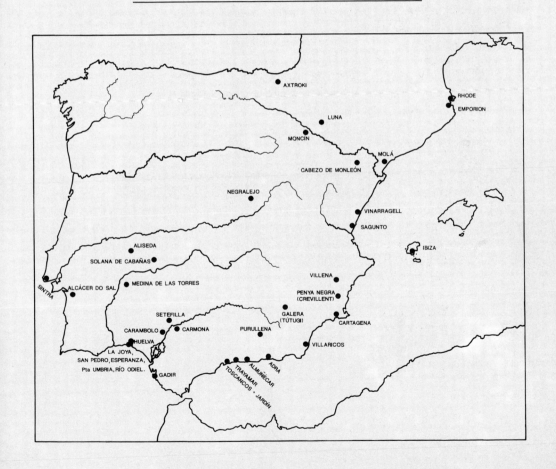

AXTROKI

RHODE

EMPORION

LUNA

MONCÍN

MOLÁ

CABEZO DE MONLEÓN

NEGRALEJO

VINARRAGELL

SAGUNTO

IBIZA

ALISEDA

SOLANA DE CABAÑAS

VILLENA

PENYA NEGRA
(CREVILLENT)

SINTRA

ALCÁCER DO SAL

MEDINA DE LAS TORRES

GALERA
(TÚTUGI)

CARTAGENA

SETEFILLA

CARAMBOLO

CARMONA

PURULLENA

VILLARICOS

HUELVA

LA JOYA,
SAN PEDRO, ESPERANZA,
Pta UMBRIA, RÍO ODIEL.

ADRA

ALMUÑÉCAR

GADIR

TRAYAMAR

TOSCANOS · JARDÍN

# 1 · Spanish landscapes

SPAIN AND PORTUGAL are the two modern political states of the Iberian Peninsula, but the exact boundary between them has always been arbitrary. The physical characteristics of this peninsula are so varied that it is justly called a miniature continent, as is Turkey at the other end of the Mediterranean Sea. The size and extent of it are deceptive, since after Switzerland it is the most mountainous region in Europe, and it is all too easy to forget how big its 595,706 sq km really are. It has a strong individuality caused by isolation and difficult terrain, and a veritable mosaic of landforms, climates and flora.

## Physical settings *(ills. 5, 6)*

The centre of the peninsula is dominated by the Castilian Meseta, or plateau, which covers roughly three-quarters of its surface, and which is split into two parts by the mountains of the Central Sierras which run from east to west. The northern Meseta lies at altitudes averaging 600–800 m, but rising to over 1200 m in the east around Soria; it tilts westwards and is drained by the river Duero, which reaches the Atlantic on the Portuguese coast at Oporto. The southern Meseta also tilts towards the west, but is some 200 m lower. All around the Mesetas are mountain ranges, save only in the southwest. These rear up into formidable barriers in the north and east in the form of the Cantabrian and Iberian mountain chains of hard limestone, pierced by few rivers or passes. To the west lies the complicated, mountainous orthography of northern Portugal, and to the south the nearly continuous wall formed by the Sierra Morena and the Penibaetic chain which shut off Andalusia. Eastwards, access to the Mediterranean is restricted by the Iberian massif which swings down to meet the Penibaetic chain behind Alicante.

On the fringes of these great ranges are narrow coastal plains. The chief ones are those along the Mediterranean coast from the Pyrenees to the Straits of Gibraltar; never more than about 20 km wide, and often as narrow as 1 km, they are largely composed of soils eroded from the nearby mountains.

In addition there are two important depressions. That of the Ebro valley in northeast Spain separates the Iberian mountains from the Pyrenees, forming a great triangle of arid territory in the rain shadow of the Pyrenees, shut off from the Mediterranean Sea by the Catalonian cordillera; the other is the valley of the Guadalquivir river in the

4 A Tartessian bronze jug from Don Benito (Badajoz), probably from a destroyed grave. It is a type which replaces the older Phoenician designs such as the piece in ill. 30.

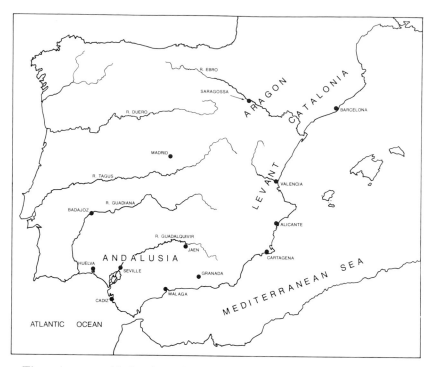

5 The main geographical regions, rivers and modern towns of the Iberian peninsula referred to in the text.

southwest, which rises in the Penibaetic chain and opens out to face the Atlantic coast. It is the opposite of the Ebro valley in almost every respect; it is fertile, well-watered, metal-rich and accessible.

Draining the peninsula are five great rivers, all except one emptying into the Atlantic Ocean. The Duero runs through the northern Meseta; the Tagus and Guadiana wind through the southern Meseta with strongly contrasting regimes; the Tagus with a fierce current often in deep gorges, emerging into the Atlantic at Lisbon; the Guadiana running sluggishly through open valleys. The Ebro river has the greatest volume of water, gives its name to the peninsula and its inhabitants, and enters the Mediterranean below Tortosa. Lastly there is the Guadalquivir in the southwest, which flows past Cordoba and Seville. None are easily navigable and all have seasons when they are charged with melt-waters and break their courses.

## Climates (*ill. 6*)

The peninsula's climates – the word must be used in the plural because there are so many distinct ones – fall into wet and dry zones. The wet ones do not concern us, especially since they are strictly confined to the north and to the Atlantic coasts of Portugal. The dry ones cover the remaining

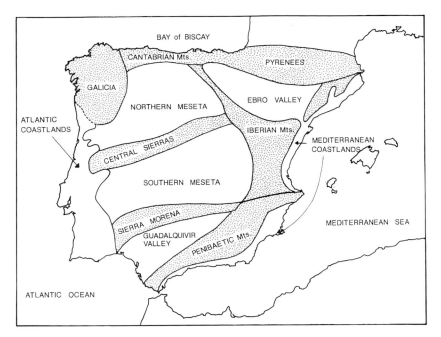

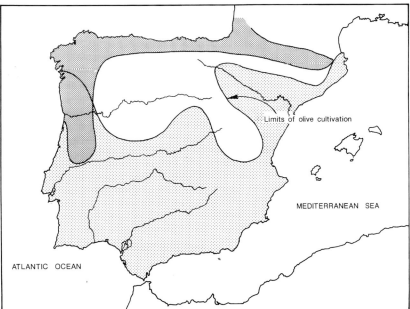

6 (*Top*) The geographical regions of the Iberian peninsula, with the mountainous chains shaded for emphasis. (*Above*) The Iberian peninsula divides neatly into wet and dry climates. The dry ones cover most of it and are shaded with a light tone; the heavier tone represents the wetter ones. The limits of Mediterranean vegetation are indicated by the boundary of modern olive trees, which cannot resist the colder, humid conditions of the north. Note that the northern Meseta has a dry climate, but is too cold for olives.

four-fifths of the peninsula and all of the regions in which the Iberians and Phoenicians lived. Essentially, there is a Mediterranean pattern to dry Spain: relatively short, wet winters, with some cold snaps including frosts at higher altitudes and inland areas, and long rainless summers from early June to late September when temperatures soar above 40 degrees C. In the interior districts this difference is exaggerated to the point where it becomes continental, and is often accompanied by strong winds. The most favoured areas for human settlement are around the Tagus estuary in Portugal, and the strip of land along the coast from Gibraltar as far north as the Pyrenees, where a benign climate reigns all year round.

As in all climates of Mediterranean character, water is relatively scarce and has a strong influence on human settlement. Rain falls mainly in late autumn and winter, rarely exceeds 600 mm in a year, and decreases brusquely towards the southeast coast. When the rains come they frequently do so in torrential storms when much water cannot be absorbed by the soil and simply runs off to be lost as floods in steep gullies. That which is absorbed frequently reappears as springs and it is these, quite as much as rivers, which have traditionally supplied human settlements.

The regions within the peninsula which interest us can be defined nicely by their climate. The *Mesetas* have a harsh, continental climate of extremes; snowy winters are followed by long, hot summers which can be quite dry for four months at a stretch. In the *Ebro valley* the climate is less rigorous in the winter, with less rainfall, but a summer as hot or hotter than that of the Mesetas. The contrast with the coastal regions is very strong: *Catalonia* in the northeast of the peninsula has a milder and moister climate than the interior, without the crude juxtaposition of Castile and Aragon; its land is more fertile and fruitful as a result. As one progresses southwards down the coast, winters become milder still, and the topography changes into a simpler one of a deep range of interior mountains fronted by a coastal plain; this is the *Levant*, with its orange groves stretching all down eastern Spain from the Ebro delta, past the Cabo de Nao in Alicante, to Murcia in the southeast. *Andalusia* is the region which covers the southern third of Spain, from the Portuguese border in the southwest to the Mediterranean coast in the southeast; it is washed by the Atlantic on the west and the Mediterranean on the east. German geographers make a felicitous distinction between 'Lower' Andalusia – the Guadalquivir valley and the Sierra Morena – and 'Upper' Andalusia, formed by the jumble of the Penibaetic mountains in the east. The climates are generally mild, wet and frost-free in winter, turning torrid in the summer; rainfall decreases markedly as one moves eastwards, and on the coasts of Almeria and Murcia there are districts which receive less than 250 mm of rainfall in an entire year, which is about 40 per cent of that which falls in the west.

## Vegetation (*ill. 6*)

Plant cover is extraordinarily varied. Botanists have identified over 5500 plants as natives. A Mediterranean flora covers 70 per cent of the land surface, and is specially adapted to the twin stresses of summer drought and great heat. The limits of this vegetation coincide closely with cultivation of the olive. The result is a flora with many perennial evergreen plants, which grows vigorously for short periods in the spring and autumn when sufficient water is available, then rests in the dry seasons. The landscapes vary tremendously from Alpine meadows on Pyrenean summits and the peaks of the Sierra Nevada in Granada, grading through beech woods, then holm oak forests, down to tough pine and juniper stands in the driest lands. In warm humid regions along the coasts the stone pine (*P. pinea*) dominates virgin woodland. In parts of Catalonia one can still see stands of evergreen holm oak (*Q. ilex*) in almost primeval luxuriance, with some trees reaching 18 m in height and protecting a dense canopied undergrowth of shrubs. This is the original climax forest. Where these splendid woodland communities have been destroyed – which is almost everywhere – they have been replaced by lower, coarser and more resistant plant cover of evergreen kermes oak scrub (*Q. coccifera*), and when even that cannot survive, by juniper bushes, rosemary, and esparto grass. In the driest parts of the country, and those with particularly poor soils denuded by erosion, aleppo pines (*P. halpensis*) have been planted in recent years in their millions, since they grow faster than autocthonous evergreen oaks; but they deplete the soil and are highly combustible.

Ancient Spain's aspect was completely different from the one upon which we now gaze. Studies of pollen grains trapped in peat bogs and charcoal from fires burned 3000 years ago show that most of the peninsula was thickly wooded with holm oak or related species, even in regions which are now treeless as far as the eye can see in all directions, such as the southern Meseta or parts of the Ebro valley. The windblown steppes are relatively recent creations. Even at the time of the Roman conquest there were still huge areas of forest over the Meseta. We do not know when these forests were definitively lost, but by the thirteenth century AD sheep-rearing on an enormous scale over Castile's wastes shows that destruction was far advanced. For the period from 1000 BC to the time of Christ, the peninsula was clothed in a far richer vegetation than we can enjoy today, and with it went all the benefits that accompany wooded land in Mediterranean conditions: a low rate of soil erosion, a constant supply of fuel, an increased water supply in springs, game animals, and soils with a higher content of humus which enhances their fertility.

With the loss of the forests came increased erosion. Since 1000 BC it can be documented dramatically. The whole of the lower Guadalquivir valley below Seville was once a great tidal gulf open to the Atlantic

Ocean. Today it is marshland criss-crossed by canals to irrigate rice fields, shut off from the sea by a barrier of coastal sand dunes. In the Ebro valley erosion since Roman times has been so intense that the whole of the Ebro delta – more than 300 sq km of land – has been built up over the last 1600 years! They are but two records of widespread degradation in their rivers' catchment areas in the interior; formerly wooded countryside is now waste, moors, heath, or in the worst cases, badlands. Yet it was not like this in the past when the Iberians lived there; nor need it remain like it for the future.

Besides its wealth of timber and forest products, the peninsula has districts with fertile soils, especially in Andalusia, the Levant, and Catalonia. Metals too have played an important part in Spain's past. The country is a storehouse of metallic wealth of all kinds; there is abundant lead and silver in the southeast close to Cartagena, and in the southwest, at the headwaters of the Rio Tinto, lies the largest mining complex in the entire Mediterranean. Here fortunes in silver were being made as early as the seventh century BC. Further inland, towards the Portuguese border and north to the Atlantic coast, cassiterite ores can be panned from shallow streams and smelted for their tin. Tin, copper and silver are also found in small pockets of ore in the southeast, actually within sight of the coast, and were worked from Bronze Age times. And in Galicia in the far northwest the Romans laid hands on the richest gold mines in their empire. Mineral wealth on this scale was a big part of the peninsula's attraction, and clearly set it apart from France, Italy, and North Africa; but how true rings the phrase coined by the American ecologist Carl O. Sauer when he wrote, 'natural resources are in fact cultural appraisals'.

# 2 · The Bronze Age mosaic

THIS OVERVIEW of the Bronze Age concentrates on one major theme: inequality, or to put it more elegantly, unequal development caused by social pressures. We can describe it through the way in which food was produced and distributed, as well as in the different modes of settlement that arose as a consequence. Some regions are occupied by nothing larger than a hamlet or grange, others have villages with estates grouped around them, while forts are distinct from both. Furthermore, there are marked divisions of wealth expressed in the form of gold jewels, carved gravestones and weaponry, that need explanations. Patterns like these are not caused by chance or incomplete fieldwork; we can be certain that these are important differences. The theme of uneven growth is developed linearly in this chapter so that we can set the scene for the first colonial contacts, which occurred around 800 BC.

## Successful economies: the full Bronze Age, 2000–1200 BC

In the later second millennium BC, Spain supported a mosaic of different farming and stockraising economies, all of them bronze-using, and well adapted to their harsh homelands. They had colonized the driest parts of the southeast, built stone 'castles' on the bleak plains of La Mancha, occupied the mountain ranges of the interior, and mined copper, tin and lead in many areas. Our interest focuses on the century between 1200 and 1100 BC, at a time when many of these groups' fortunes changed dramatically. Some failed to survive at all, other, hardier ones chose fresh localities for their villages in the same regions: the patterns of life that had flourished since 2000 BC became extinct over wide regions. Everywhere these changes can be attested there is a corresponding trend towards a more uniform material culture that replaces the older styles: the flint tools, pottery and metal artefacts are common over much larger areas than before.

The older Bronze Age societies had been extremely successful. In the southeast simple irrigation farming in the river bottoms was established before 2200 BC; we can see this from the placement of the villages, and still more directly from the types of plants that were cultivated. They include wheat, barley, grape and almond, all well adapted to dry soils, but also flax, which needs lots of water if its cultivation is to be worthwhile. The fat flax seeds from sites in the southeast come from irrigated crops.

In the mountains behind Valencia and Cuenca a pattern of scattered hamlets and crofts shows that sheep rearing, with its essential seasonal transhumance, was organized. Of especial interest here is the movement of sheep from summer pastures in the mountains to winter ones at lower altitudes, either on the Mediterranean coast around Valencia, or inland towards La Mancha. The harsh winters make it impossible to keep sheep overwinter unless they are stabled, so transhumance is the farmer's best solution. Movement like this would integrate diverse regions into one economic system, each part dependent upon the other.

One reason for this achievement in the drier parts of the peninsula may have been adroit forms of stock management, some of which we can deduce from the animal bones found in the larger settlements. Stockraising has always been exceptionally important in Spain, since it is the only way that much of the countryside can be exploited; it is too dry for effective cereal growing, or the droughts strike too frequently, or the forage for animals is confined to one region for a few months only. In historical times, the answer has been to keep animals in great numbers, often to the detriment of arable farming. This is an exaggerated pattern, but it does show that Spain can be productive when exploited by herding or grazing regimes. Less extreme, but still specialized, herding economies in the Bronze Age around 1500–1200 BC show it was the animals' milk, manure and tractive power that was appreciated, as well as their meat.

Of course, much meat was eaten, but when detailed examinations of animal remains are carried out in order to form a picture of their population structure in terms of age and sex, and so on, some important differences begin to emerge. For instance at the village of Cerro de la Encina (Granada) there is evidence of horses having been trained both for riding and transport, and surprisingly enough, cows were kept for their milk and cheese on the plains of La Mancha at Azuer and Los Palacios. Sheep are everywhere important, more so in dry country than elsewhere, and were probably kept for their milk, fertilizer and mutton rather than their wool; woolly breeds do not appear until 800 BC. Pigs too, were found on nearly all sites, but in very small numbers, perhaps only a couple of sows with their piglets. Their great popularity 500 years before never returned. These are all choices made for social reasons as far as we can judge; that is, there is no sharp climatic change, or population increase, that would make pig-raising expensive and favour sheep accordingly. These economic practices would make best sense to the farmer if he knew that he could trade his surplus animals for something else that he lacked, and as a working hypothesis, this picture of increasing specialization in animal labour and secondary products does account for the evident prosperity of the times (ill. 7).

Radical change struck in the twelfth century. Evidence indicates that the villages, landscapes and burial customs end sharply, and there is no

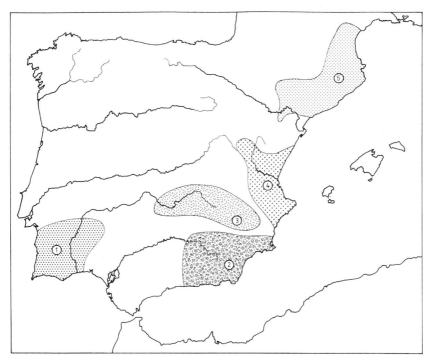

7 Regional Bronze Age cultural groups in Spain and Portugal between 1500 and 1200 BC. *1* the Southwest; *2* the Argaric group. *3* the Motillas of the Southern Meseta; *4* the Valencian or Levantine group; *5* the Catalonian and Southwest French group.

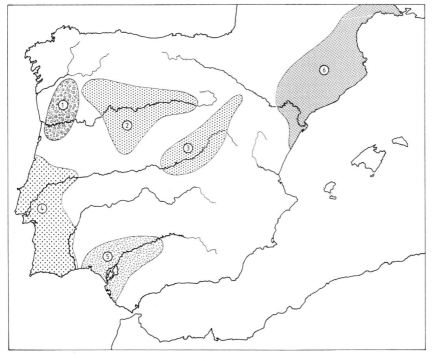

8 A distribution map of major groups of decorated pottery of the later Bronze Age, around 900 BC: *1* North Portugal, Penha style wares; *2* Old Castile, Boquique style wares; *3* New Castile, Boquique style wares; *4* Central and south Portugal, pattern-burnished pottery; *5* Western Andalusian pattern-burnished pottery; *6* Catalonian Urnfield pottery.

27

obvious cause like an epidemic or lengthy drought. The most likely reason is not a catastrophic one at all, but something within the societies themselves, something which caused a complete realignment in new patterns.

### Realignments after 1200 BC

Our material for the later Bronze Age can be organized into two phases from 1200 to 900 and 900 to 700 BC respectively. At this point we enter into the orientalizing period, which is discussed in Chapter 4. The transformation of the older Bronze Age societies occurs in the choice of new sites for villages, different styles of housing, and a preference for pottery of open shape. It occurs about the same time in the region of Andalusia in the south and on both Mesetas; that is, over much of 'dry' Spain (*ill. 8*).

Farming settlements become common on both Mesetas after 1100 BC, and people desert the rock shelters, caves and defended sites in favour of villages on open river terraces alongside the best cereal-growing lands. This can be seen in the Duero valley in the provinces of Zamora and Salamanca, as well as in the fertile region between Madrid and Guadalajara on the southern Meseta. Many were short-lived villages, perhaps occupied for a generation, like Negralejo and Arenero de Soto (Madrid), which are like another hundred in this class. They were provided with large grain silos, later backfilled with household rubbish, although the houses that once stood there have vanished entirely under the farmers' ploughs. Better preserved settlements like the one at Moncín (Borja, Zaragoza) help us to complete the picture. Originally, the silos were capable of holding up to two tons of grain each, enough food for four adults for two years. An undamaged settlement was discovered at the Cerro de la Encina (Monachil, Granada). Here houses were found with stuccoed walls, ornamented with geometric patterns, cobbled floors for looms, and oval grain bins lined with stones. The open shapes of pottery seem to be intended to display food more than before, so there may have been a change in eating habits, or perhaps in the food itself; more roast and baked meats, or cereal made into cakes rather than porridge, could account for this.

All this looks like an increasing population sustained by successful grain cultivation being added to its older staples of livestock. In order to provide this cereal, the cornlands must have been ploughed, and for that plough teams would have been essential. Unlike irrigation, where hand labour with hoes is normal, dry farming needs plough teams to till extensive areas of soil for sowing wheat or barley. Hoeing makes no impression at all on dry soils, so the Meseta expansion is to be linked with a more ready availability of draught oxen. It is also interesting that the grain silos, insignificant clues in themselves, are the first large storage units for food to be found on the Mesetas, and we know they could keep grain edible for at least twenty years. These accumulated food stocks may have been the source of the sudden enrichment of the archaeological record on the Mesetas, and it is tempting to link them with the abandonment of the older forts in the southeast and La Mancha. These changes occupy a far larger world than just one region, or one vegetation zone.

Metal artefacts for this time are scarce everywhere, and jewels still rarer. By contrast, the ability to work bronze is very widespread, and small tools, flat axes and arrowheads are common, even though the weight of metal actually available is low. The only moulds known are all made of stone, and the metal alloys still include copper mixed with arsenic to harden it. The best gold jewellery comes from the southwest, in a hoard weighing 1.55 kg found in a pot at Bodonal de la Sierra (Badajoz), with gold torcs linked to those made at the same time in Ireland. Indeed, this hoard may well contain pieces of Irish manufacture. However, in general so little metal was in circulation that basic tools for everyday use were still made from flint, and even the coarsest material was pressed into service. There is a wide range of tools for cutting, chopping, and scraping, probably for cleaning hides, as well as reaping tools, or at least the flint inserts for curved sickles used for cereal harvesting. These show no change in their basic shape from flint sickles 800 years older. Some sites have hundreds of flint tools, and even as late as 800 BC they are widely used; Moncín is one example with over 400 sickles and another 600 flint tools from the period 1200–1000 BC. The evidence for metal scarcity could not be plainer. For the whole of the Bronze Age, flint, not metal, was used for the most basic farming tools. Metal farming implements do not appear in Mediterranean Spain until iron becomes widely available after 600 BC.

Our picture of this period is enriched by the outstanding funerary monuments of the southwest, especially southern Portugal, associated with cemeteries of cist graves. There is continuity of burial rite from 1800 to 650 BC and later, and the region does not show the profound changes in the twelfth century that affected the Mesetas and Andalusia. This may be because so few villages have been systematically excavated, but the grave lots do make an unbroken series. The grave stelas occur in the later part of the southwest Bronze Age, beginning about 1300 BC, and continue, with changes in their decoration, until replaced with ones carrying a written script after 650 BC (*ill. 9*). They were originally set up above the graves of distinguished or wealthy people, probably men, and show a warlike panoply of hafted axes, swords, daggers, and enigmatic objects like an anchor (*ill. 10*). None of these items has yet been found buried in a cist grave, which usually held more modest offerings of pottery and personal ornaments, but they are known elsewhere in the south and southeast of Spain.

## Setting the scene for colonial contacts

The succeeding period from 900 to 700 BC is an intensification of the patterns set up before and there are villages all over Andalusia, and in the Levant and Ebro valley, that give an accurate chronology of events. The period is marked out as well by distinctive pottery, grandiose gold jewellery and tableware, and a glut of bronze weaponry.

Of the economy we know surprisingly little, other than its success, which is evident from the villages. In Andalusia the settlement plans tell us rather more than in the previous period, since there are single-period ones like Peñón de la Reina (Alboloduy, Almería) to examine. This site was on a high, steep hill, surrounded by a stout stone wall, and had oval houses scattered inside without any formal planning: no central street, citadel, square or water hole. Nevertheless, the finds were not poor.

A more impressive village is currently being excavated at the Cuesta del Negro (Purullena, Granada) where the houses are rectangular, and another at the Cerro del Real (Galera, Granada), where the most interesting late Bronze Age house of all was found. This village occupies a flat-topped promontory, flanked by deep gullies, overlooking the little Galera river and its market gardens. The oval house that was uncovered measures 11.5 by 7 m; it was built of big rectangular mud bricks, all

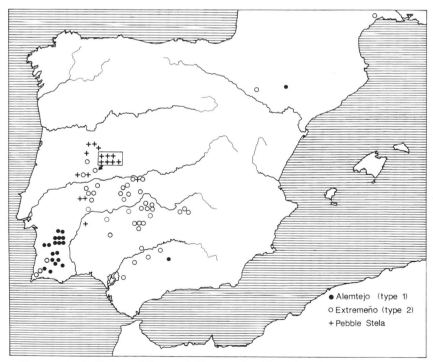

Alemtejo (type 1)
Extremeño (type 2)
Pebble Stela

9 Grave stelas in Spain and Portugal. Type 1, the oldest, dates between 1300 and 900 BC; type 2 is later, between 900 and 650 BC, and its latest examples carry inscriptions.

regularly sized, and mortared together with clay, then finished off on both faces with coloured plaster and clay wash. The eaves projected to form a sheltered portico all around, and the roof was held up by three mud-brick pillars and three wooden posts. Inside was a bench to hold jars, a small pantry to one side, and a central fireplace. But what caught the excavators' attention was the remarkable attention to cleanliness that the inhabitants had lavished on the place. It was regularly whitewashed inside, and the floor swept clean and strewn with fine sand; some twenty lenses of sand were found interfingered with the layers of whitewash that accumulated at the curved base of the walls. Its size is twice that of normal houses, and the scrupulous cleanliness makes it unusual also. It might not be an ordinary dwelling at all, not even of a wealthy person, but a building for public reunions, perhaps a meeting house for the village elders. Whatever our views, it is a uniquely fine construction for its period, and the only building for which a public use can be suggested.

Expansion into the Spanish Levant is shown by newly discovered villages near the Mediterranean coast. None have been excavated extensively because their deposits are so deep and complicated, but we can form a picture of what happened in the period 1200–700 BC, which until ten years ago was a complete blank. The Valencian region, both the mountainous interior and the accessible coast, escaped the changes that affected the Meseta and Andalusia. The later Bronze Age finds are sporadic, intrusive, and usually from well-defended sites; the house plans and pottery are unlike those used before in the Valencian Bronze Age. We must note too that cultural material before 800 BC is very scarce indeed, and the best view of the new developments is only a partial one from the settlement at Vinarragell (Burriana, Castellón de la Plana), sited on a small eminence alongside the river Millares. It was occupied from 800 to 450 BC, and above the oldest level, of Andalusian affinities, was another with decorated pottery related to the types in Catalonia. Above that were Phoenician potsherds of the sixth century. The other important village is at the Penya Negra (Crevillent, Alicante), which is similar to Vinarragell, but has better preserved houses. Here, oval ones are replaced by large rectangular buildings fitted with a pantry and central hearth, very much in the style of those common in Aragon and Catalonia in the eighth century. Nothing is known of the burial customs.

In the southwest the period 900–700 BC is marked out by the use of pottery ornamented with burnished patterns, some of it exceedingly elaborate and fine. The regional styles are the luxury ceramics of the period.

Grave stelas gain in popularity and richness, and not only become widespread in the southwest, but also provide us with a wealth of detail which would otherwise be lost to view (*ill. 10*). These are usually single flat stones, and nearly all are chance finds without original contexts. In a few cases, several have been found together, as at Valencina de Alcántara

10–12 **Stone stelas** (*Above*) A grave stela from Assento (Beja, Portugal), bearing hafted axes, a sheathed sword and an enigmatic object like a double-ended anchor. This style of stela is confined to southern Portugal and dates between 1300 and 900 BC. (*Right*) A stela from Solana de Cabañas (Logrosán, Cáceres) which had been erected above a warrior's grave. It dates between 850 and 750 BC. (*Far right*) On the northernmost edge of the stelas' distribution is the find from Luna (Zaragoza), of the period 800–650 BC. It is a sandstone block 1.33 m tall, trimmed roughly to human shape, and depicts a fancy round shield at the top, and a complicated musical instrument below, probably a lyre, with decorated soundbox and slight horns to spread the strings correctly. The nearest parallels are Phoenician musical instruments, and this may be a direct copy of one of them. Is it capricious to see these emblems as those of a warrior with musical tastes?

and Torrejón de Rubio, each with three stelas, as if there had once been an important cemetery there. The one from Solana de Cabañas (Logrosán, Cáceres) was associated with a single grave cut into the bedrock and covered with a heap of loose stones (*ill. 11*). All of these stelas developed from the older, more restrained ones in the Algarve, and often depict the warrior as an ungainly little stick figure, surrounded by his prized possessions: bronze shields, slashing swords, helmets, four-wheeled carts, two-wheeled chariots, and even small details like his favourite brooch, belt buckle and mirror. These objects are sufficiently well drawn to be recognizable from artefacts found in the same area, and

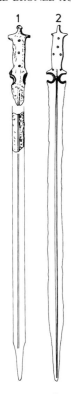

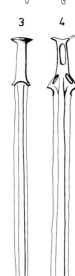

their depiction on the grave slabs emphasizes the individual wealth of their owners. There are no overtly ritual or cult symbols for us to speculate about; all is concrete, particular, and highly materialistic, with a minimum of symbolism, if any at all. There are even a few attempts to show a scene. The stela from Ategua (Cordoba) has the deceased 'hero' shown as a giant with his shield and spear, with seven tiny slaves in two groups below him, and another two slaves, one of whom is dead, at his feet. He also has the services of a two-wheeled chariot drawn by a pair of horses and with a charioteer. Musical instruments were appreciated too, as we can see from the lyre carved on the slab from Luna (Zaragoza) (*ill. 12*).

The range of these objects stresses novelties, imported fashions, and weaponry. The carts and chariots are the oldest wheeled vehicles in Iberia, and their arrival, like the lyre, is due to Phoenician imports appearing in the region after 800 BC. The oldest objects date to the period 850–800 BC, and the latest ones to around 650 BC; the shields and brooches are types that were current in Cyprus in the ninth century and originate from there. The slashing swords and helmets belong to the Atlantic tradition of bronze working, as do the heavy spearheads. Identical weapons have been found in the shipwreck cargo from the Río Odiel at Huelva, radiocarbon-dated to about 850 BC.

The final group of grave markers is on the margins of the main distribution, and is distinguished by its use of small river boulders less than 1 m high, depicting a single central figure. These figures usually have an elaborate headdress or crown, with heavy collars, perhaps gold one such as that from Sintra, rather than a miscellaneous collection of novelties scattered around them. The boulder stelas have been interpreted as part of the paraphernalia of a sacred chieftainship, with the dead leader depicted with objects that invest him with power, rather than possessions that assert his status as a rich warrior. Their iconography is clearly different from the other stelas and requires some explanation of this type; we would learn much if we could excavate a cemetery in which these boulder carvings were in their original settings.

As a group, the stelas are an impressive statement of the degree to which oriental ideas marked the wealthier social strata in the later Bronze Age.

Another category of new possessions in the southwest is the bronze weaponry of Atlantic type (*ill. 13*). This is made of true tin bronze, that is, copper alloyed with 8–10 per cent tin, and consists of designs like those of West European weapons intended for fighting on horseback with a long

*13 (Left)* Heavy weaponry from southern Spain. Four swords of styles common at the end of the Bronze Age in the eighth to the seventh centuries. *1* Iron sword from Estacar de Robarinas (Cástulo, Jaén); *2* Bronze sword like no. 1, but from Alcalá del Río (Seville); *3* Metal-hilted sword from the hoard dredged from the Río Odiel at Huelva; *4* Atlantic style of bronze sword also from the Río Odiel hoard.

slashing sword, or hand to hand at close quarters with a more pointed instrument to pierce the joints between body armour. There is also a lot of horse tackle from the same sources, as well as scraps from bronze helmets. For the first time, metalwork is now found in hoards, with scrap being collected for recycling; before this, hoarding of metal was virtually unknown in Mediterranean Spain. It, too, is an Atlantic trait, probably connected with the reorganization of the metal supply routes along the Atlantic seaboards of Iberia and France, and stretching as far as southeast England. The 'carp's tongue complex', which takes its name from the distinctive stabbing point of the sword in the group of weapons traded through the coastal regions, was established by 900 BC and its centre was located around the Loire estuary in France. There is a scatter of imported bronze swords in the southwest and south of the peninsula from 1200 BC, but Atlantic metalwork only becomes common after 900 BC.

The greatest find, and one crucial for the entire Atlantic bronze industry, is from a shipwreck cargo dredged from the bed of the Río Odiel in Huelva harbour, in 1923. It comprises more than 400 objects, and many more were probably lost at the time of discovery. There are over 260 complete weapons: 78 swords, mostly carp's tongue types, 29 daggers, 90 spearheads, 62 spear butts, and another 100 smaller pieces of bronze brooches, arrowheads, buttons, woodworking tools, needles, rivets from helmets, and scrap. All analysed metal is 10 per cent tin bronze. The cargo contains objects already obsolete and at least a century old when it was assembled, but the date can be accurately determined by the radiocarbon dates of wood from the spearhead sockets to about 850 BC, and from the brooches current around the same time in Cyprus. The date for the cargo is therefore between 850 and 800 BC. This is important because it records the episode when Atlantic metalwork began to be collected into hoards and spread along the southern coast of Spain and then as far as Sardinia and Italy. This trail marks the route which opened before 800 BC and which looks as though it was itself stimulated by Phoenician enterprises at a time immediately before their settlements at Gadir (Cadiz) and on the Malaga coast.

Contemporary with these foreign bronzes are hoards of gold jewellery, rich even by the extravagant standards of later times. The artefacts are all personal jewels, especially heavy gold collars and plain bracelets. The most gorgeous example is that from Sintra (Portugal) (*ill. 14*). Other notable ones were found at Sagrajas (Badajoz), recovered from a small oval house that had burned down. This treasure comprised a double collar with an ingenious closing segment, weighing just over 2 kg, and five small bracelets with a couple of bits of twisted gold wire. A little more informative is the treasure from Berzocana (Cáceres), where two decorated gold collars were hidden inside a sheet bronze bowl in the eighth century. But none of these can begin to match the astonishing gold treasure recovered in December 1963 at Villena (Alicante) (*ills. 15, 16*).

14 The collar with locking plate from Sintra (Portugal) is an outstanding example of goldsmith's work in the ninth century.

The treasure was discovered in time to excavate it under controlled conditions, and to be certain that no pieces were 'lost'. This cache, weighing 9.75 kg, included sixty-six metal objects and an amber bead; all except six of the metal objects were gold. From the day of its discovery it has attracted immense public interest, yet it is little known outside Spain. The treasure was found in a large clay jar, buried by itself in river gravels outside the town of Villena. It was hidden deliberately in an isolated spot, and the gold was all neatly packed into the jar like crockery in an old-fashioned china barrel. There are three components to the hoard: 28 gold bracelets, mostly decorated; 11 gold bowls and 5 flagons of gold and silver; 14 smaller pieces from jewels and dresses, as well as fittings from a wooden casket.

In other words, this represents a hoard of jewellery far greater than any one person could have worn, with a dinner service of the richest kind, and a few precious scraps ripped off clothing and furniture. Twenty-three of the bracelets have deep mouldings and rows of projecting teeth like gearwheels, and are of a type developed in the southwest of the peninsula; their presence in the Villena hoard is as exotic, imported gold finery. The open bowls are all profusely decorated with geometric patterns brought out by rows of embossed dots, in a style closely matched in central Germany, and paralleled by two others found in roadworks at Axtroki (Guipúzcoa) in the Basque region. The flasks are unique to the hoard, but might be the inspirations for the delicate clay bottles made at this time and placed in cist graves in the southwest; two are gold, and three of

15, 16 **The Villena hoard** (*Top*) Gold jugs and massive bracelets. (*Above*) Gold bowls decorated with designs made with raised bosses, and more massive gold bracelets.

silver, with raised mouldings to make a pleasing decoration. The other pieces are of the highest interest, for they include an iron knob or rivet, decorated with gold foil. It is the presence of this piece, and a small iron ring, which indicates that this hoard was buried towards the end of the eighth century, around 750 to 700 BC, since iron was completely unknown in the peninsula until introduced by the Phoenicians. This is not to deny that there are older pieces in the hoard, but to establish that its burial could not have been earlier than this date. These are the oldest iron pieces in Spain, and the metal was obviously being treated as a commodity as precious as gold itself, hence its decoration and inclusion in the hoard.

Villena is an exceptionally rich treasure, and is interesting as a standard against which to measure the scale of wealth that could have been attached to some of the chieftains of the Spanish Levant. But since this is not an area especially favoured with natural resources or metals, the varied nature of the cache, especially the imported bracelets, makes one wonder if this hoard is not, in fact, loot from raids rather than a local chieftain's fortune.

To complete the panorama of the later Bronze Age in Mediterranean Spain, we must turn to Catalonia and the Ebro valley. Here is a distinctive group of cemeteries and settlements belonging to the Central European tradition of Urnfields, cultures characterized by cremation burial in biconical pots, in shallow pits or under little mounds. The simple settlements of rectangular houses, and scanty bronze metalwork follow local tastes. The cemeteries can be arranged in an unbroken series from 1100 to 550 BC, beginning with Can Missert (Tarrasa, Barcelona), followed by Agullana (Gerona) which spans the period 1100–600 BC with nearly 700 burials. The transition to iron-using is best seen at the joint village and cemetery of El Molà (Falset, Tarragona). The settlement of rectangular houses occupies a low hill 100 by 30 m in extent, and has a shallow stratigraphy indicative of a short occupation. Most of the tools were made of flint, and basalt was used for axes since metal was too precious to employ in this manner. Downslope lay a little cemetery of 172 graves, all clustered in an area less than 20 by 15 m. Two relatively rich graves, one with thirty-eight and another with forty-five thin bronze bracelets came to light, but at least one-fifth of the other graves had some metal grave goods, showing that wealth, if that is what we can call it, was widely distributed in this society. On the edges of the cemetery, in positions that were later than the other graves, were four burials with iron objects, mainly small knives and an iron ring. The bronze brooches and iron objects date El Molà to between 700 and 550 BC.

The economic structures are hard to discern anywhere in the Urnfield cultures, but from the siting of villages high up in the Pyrenees, deep inside the mountain chain, as well as inland on the dry plains of Urgel and Los Monegros, it is obvious that livestock was really important. These areas are best exploited by transhumant livestock, grazing in the

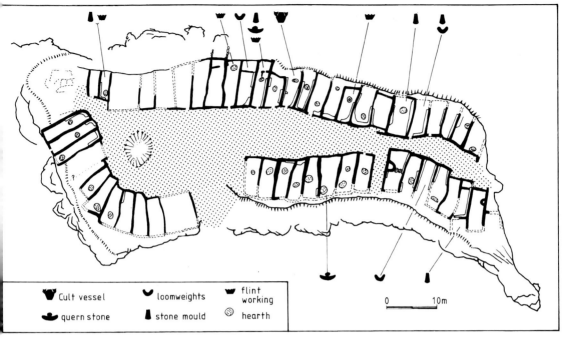

17 Completely excavated villages of the Bronze Age are rare. This example of
around 800 BC from the Cabezo de Monleón (Zaragoza) is especially clear, with
blocks of rooms forming dwelling and workshop units on both sides of the central
street. The position of the main classes of artefact is shown.

mountains in the summer and overwintering on the plains where heavy
rains and slight frosts bring early pastures. This economic com-
plementarity lasted until recent years, and is a pattern that is also
reflected in the many cave sites that have Urnfield pottery in their levels.
They are located in areas of grazing rather than arable land. Social
stratification seems at a rudimentary level, with nothing comparable to
that established in Andalusia and the southwest; there are no big fortified
sites, no rich burials, important metal hoards, gold treasures, or even
villages with deep layers of soil that attest a long period of occupation in
one place.

In the Ebro valley the village of Cabezo de Monleón (Caspe, Zaragoza)
gives the best information that we have on the daily life and social
organization of this time (*ill. 17*). The settlement occupies a flat-topped
hill 5 km from the river Ebro, in an exceptionally arid region. The hilltop
is similar in size to the site of El Molà. Complete excavation exposed fifty-
seven rooms arranged around a central street, with a pond at one end.
The rooms are part of larger dwelling units, not complete houses in
themselves; the finds inside them show that the basic crafts proper to an
agricultural life based on dry farming, were carried out here. At least
eight activity groups stand out, and crafts are not restricted to one room

or house, as might have been expected. Before the gateway into the village is the wealthiest residence, with the only evidence for ritual, recognized by a cult vessel with four miniature vases attached to its rim to receive libations. But the fact that several people were capable of casting bronze, flaking stone implements, and weaving cloth does show that specialization was rudimentary, notwithstanding the more prosperous residence opposite the gateway. The Cabezo de Monleón has much handmade pottery decorated in Urnfield fashion, and stone moulds for simple bronze rings, a spearhead and lugged flat axe; all these can be dated to around 800 BC. This was still an entirely bronze-using economy, with flint in everyday use.

Our overall impression of the regular architecture, the utter lack of barns, stables or central food stores of any kind, and the absence of public spaces or cult rooms, is of a homogeneous society with few social differences of a material kind. This agrees with the finds from the cemetery at El Molà, which are slightly later in date.

## Conclusions

Reviewing this later Bronze Age panorama from the Algarve to Aragon on the eve of the first colonizations, one is struck by four things. There is diversity in social gradings from one region to another which is unconnected with population density or settlement size: the southwest stands out above all other areas with its grave monuments and millennial tradition of authority. Next, the technological poverty of Mediterranean Spain even as late as 800 BC, is notable. Only with the injection of Atlantic bronze-working skills into the southwest, and to a much lesser degree into Catalonia and its Urnfield culture, does real tin bronze become available in quantity, and a truly effective offensive weaponry appear. The lack of hoarded metal, the small amount of copper, lead or gold actually circulating or consumed in burials, is confirmed by the widespread use of flint and stone tools for daily tasks. Thirdly, there is a clear lack of accumulated wealth to attract traders from afar; most of the gold treasures date after 800 BC, and the largest of them, Villena, actually had iron objects. Finally, the relatively low population densities, the small, usually undefended villages, continue a pattern which began in the twelfth century, when the citadels of the older Bronze Age societies were slighted. Iberia at the end of the Bronze Age was not an 'El Dorado', and this conclusion will carry weight in helping us to understand why, and how, the first colonizations by Phoenicians and Greeks took place, and the orientalizing imitations they inspired.

# 3 · Phoenician colonies in Spain

HISTORICAL TRADITION credits the Phoenicians with voyages to southern Spain in the twelfth century BC and places the foundation of their base at Gadir (Cadiz) around 1100 BC, by a fleet which sailed from Tyre. A few years later was founded Utica, close to Carthage on the African coast. Of these endeavours we know very little indeed, since it is in their nature that the first colonial contacts would be brief and slight. One does not expect archaeological traces of them, and that is exactly the case with the first Phoenician presence in the far west. The historical sources still stand alone, and unverified. There were Phoenicians in the tenth century on Crete, and in the eleventh on Sardinia, but it is after 800 BC that evidence really begins to accumulate for their activity in southern Spain. These great sea voyages were not undertaken haphazardly. They were the product of the peculiar political status of the Phoenician cities in the eastern Mediterranean, especially Tyre and Byblos, and their position as vassals of the Assyrian empire from the ninth century onwards.

The trading cities on the Phoenician coast (now part of modern Lebanon) were part of the political economy first of the Egyptian empire, then, after 1100 BC, of the Assyrians, and their relations with these states governed their behaviour. The Phoenician cities provided services and goods to their powerful neighbours, in return for protection, access to profitable markets, and foodstuffs. As maritime powers, they were ideally placed to forge alliances with inland empires, act as intermediaries, and organize regional trading systems to their advantage. It is in these circumstances that the Phoenician colonization of the central and western Mediterranean took place, and where motives can be discovered. The pace and intensity of contact quicken after 900 BC when Phoenician cities came to specialize in the manufacture of luxury goods: dyed clothes, embroidery, glassware and metal vessels, inlaid furniture, perfumes, and rare foods.

One powerful attraction of the west lay in its untapped metal lodes, especially tin, silver, and gold, for which there was an inexhausitble demand in the Orient. Silver, especially, was needed since the Assyrians used a silver standard for many commercial transactions, including credit and loans, which lay at the heart of their economy. This expanded greatly in the late eighth century BC after Assyrian victories over the Urartians who had controlled trade routes to Syria and the northwest for more than a hundred years. One consequence of this was that the Phoenicians were required to become leading suppliers of primary raw materials, as well as finished manufactures, and these new demands from their overlords forced them to extend their trade simply to survive. This increased Assyrian demand for raw materials changed the whole scale of Phoenician production, and it is in this enlarged Mediterranean world after 710 BC that the metals from the far west became so significant. This, briefly, is a summary of the attractive hypothesis of the British archaeologist, Susan Frankenstein; it gives the setting in which colonial contact was made in southern Spain, and the broad reasons behind it. The Phoenician city states took on the role as agents of Assyrian power.

The pattern of Phoenician trade was linked to specialist production centres, connecting different areas and political systems which otherwise would not have been drawn together, and establishing a rate of exchange much to their own advantage. They could do this fairly easily since they had a monopoly on both the specialized manufactures that everyone desired, and the marine transport, so they could stimulate demand where they chose to do so. A virgin market was the ideal since it could be scoured hard for huge profits; this accounts for their interest in Spain, especially in the silver mines behind Huelva in the Río Tinto, and near Cástulo in the Sierra Morena. The Phoenicians were able to locate new metal sources, and unlock the wealth from them, unhindered, for a century and a half.

The traders worked through a system of Phoenician family firms, who had representatives in their home town in the eastern Mediterranean as well as in their new markets and factories; they owned their own ships, too, and were prepared to take risks which their overlords could not well calculate, or were unwilling to do, and so profited greatly.

The trail of the Phoenicians can be followed to Sardinia in the eleventh century, where Semitic inscriptions from Nora show their presence. The longest inscription dates from the reign of King Pygmalion of Tyre (831–785 BC), detailing a successful expedition that he had sent out around 825 BC. A fragment of an even older inscription, dated by its letter forms to the eleventh century by the Semitic epigraphist Frank Moore Cross, shows how early Phoenician interest was in Sardinia. From this base, onward journeys to Spain were relatively simple. The bronze statuettes of the twelfth to the eleventh centuries from Sciacca near Selinunte (in Sicily) and the Temple of Melkart at Sancti Petri (Cadiz) are chance finds dredged from the seabed that could mark the route. All portray the Semitic god Reshef, the smiter.

Beyond Sardinia, Phoenician enterprise in the far west falls into two periods. The older one starts around 800 BC and joins trading systems along the Atlantic seaboard that had already existed in the later Bronze Age. This network extended as far as Ireland and northwest Europe, and the richer objects circulating in it were engraved on the stone stelas of the southwest. This pre-existing circuit must have sorely tempted the Phoenicians who first encountered it, since they tapped it so fruitfully;

the cargo of bronze from the shipwreck in Huelva harbour belongs to this cycle of exchange. Scattered Atlantic bronzes, mainly palstave axes and carp's tongue swords, are scattered in a trail all across southern Spain, into Ibiza and the Balearics, and then end in substantial hoards in Sardinia, such as Monte Sa Idda and Forraxi Nioi.

## Colonial prosperity

The second period of Phoenician involvement has a different level of commitment, and is more intense than before. Armed with knowledge gained over three generations, Phoenician trading firms from Tyre and Sidon set up permanent colonial posts where they manufactured finished luxuries as well as iron objects, cloth, dyes, and foodstuffs like oil and wine. This is reflected in the increased quantities of Phoenician luxuries in Spain after 700 BC, and the powerful indigenous reaction to them; this is the orientalizing episode, which is discussed shortly. It is also the moment when silver-working at the Río Tinto mines gets into full swing. This second stage coincides closely with Assyrian reliance upon Phoenician supplies of vital raw materials, and ends abruptly with their defeat by the Babylonians in 612 BC. Subsequently, the Phoenician cities are absorbed entirely into the new empire and their commerce with the far west curtailed by 573 BC. It is these far-reaching events in the Orient which made possible Carthage's supremacy over all other Semitic colonies in the west. There was also freer and more competitive access to Iberian riches at the end of the seventh century BC, as the value of silver fell in the east, and from this time Greek interest in the peninsula awakens.

Choosing sites for colonial settlement followed a consistent pattern, and despite changes in Spanish coastal geography over the last 3000 years, such as the silting up of the Huelva estuary, or, on a huge scale, the formation of the marshlands in the lower Guadalquivir valley downstream from Seville, these Phoenician preferences are still identifiable. The essential combination included a sheltered anchorage for their ships, fresh water, sufficient arable land for subsistence farming, and an eminence, which need not be more than a few metres high, for the colony itself (*ill. 18*). Low hillocks, offshore islands or rocky headlands jutting into the sea were selected, and scores of suitable sites can be found on the south Spanish coast, from Cadiz in the west to Adra (Almeria) in the east. Reasonable communication with the interior was valued, too. The early colonies cluster around Malaga, but this is simply the region where most modern work has been carried out, and surely many others will be discovered on the coast from Marbella to Gibraltar, and thence northwest to Cadiz.

The successful study of this colonial system is indebted to the work of the German archaeologists Hermanfrid Schubart and H-G. Niemeyer,

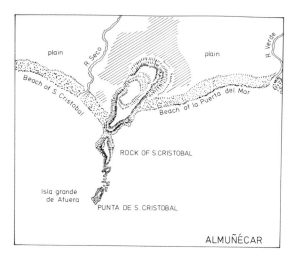

18 Almuñécar has all the characteristics of the coastal sites that Phoenician colonists sought most eagerly. It was a small, steep, isolated promontory jutting out into the sea which would make a safe base; the sandy beaches allowed boats to be drawn up easily on either side of rocks, which gave shelter in contrary winds. Fresh water and fertile soil were immediately at hand, too. The modern town is shown as a shaded area.

19 A view from the colony of Toscanos (Malaga), looking northwest out over the estuary of the Río Vélez towards the Mediterranean. In the eighth century the landscape was quite different since an inlet of the sea reached the foot of the low hills selected for settlement.

whose patient excavations of half a dozen settlements and cemeteries on the Malaga coast since 1964 have discovered things which were barely imaginable thirty years ago, and which quite transform our understanding of the Phoenicians in the far west.

The sites around the estuary of the Río Vélez in Malaga make the best starting point to see what Phoenician colonies looked like, and did, 2700 years ago.

The colony of Toscanos occupied a low hill, 12 m above the estuary of the Río Vélez, and was settled around 750 BC (*ill. 19*). This evidently did well, and by 700 BC entered upon a long period of prosperity that lasted until 550 BC, when it was abandoned. The *floruit* coincided with the construction of a fine stone warehouse, measuring at least 11 by 15 m, with three naves, one of them two stories high reached by an outside staircase. Although one compartment had many Phoenician storage amphoras in it, the close date of its use was provided by the Greek pottery such as the Attic *SOS* amphoras (which take their name from a distinctive band of painted decoration on the neck which is like the letters *SOSOS* [*ill. 45*]) and sherds from protocorinthian handled bowls. The

exact use of the building, which was clearly one of the largest in the colony and important, is not clear, but it was likely a storage depot for merchandise, a counting house too, perhaps for traders; that is, it had a semi-public position in the settlement. Domestic houses associated with the storehouse included at least three substantial dwellings of prosperous owners, and three more for much humbler families, perhaps the attendants who served the depot.

The colony was protected at this time by a deep ditch on the landward side, which probably had a wooden palisade or rampart behind it for extra strength. The climax of Toscanos's prosperity came after 650 BC, when the colony expanded to its greatest size. To make room for it, the defensive ditch was filled in, and settlement spread up the slopes of the neighbouring hill of Alarcón, whose summit is 79 m high. There may also have been growth to the nearby Cerro del Peñón, which would have to be included in any defensive perimeter to make the colony secure. A strong but serviceable wall of rough stonework and mud brick was erected by 600 BC around Alarcón. If the occupation did indeed cover the slopes of both hills, and the spaces in between them – or even only part of it – the colony would have been of considerable size. The latest estimates of Professor Niemeyer are for a population of 1000–1500 persons. Its prosperity faded soon after these changes, however, and by 550 BC it was abandoned, not to be reoccupied until Roman times. Monumental stone buildings in distinctive Phoenician masonry were built at Toscanos, but most were dismantled and their blocks reused in the Roman period, so we cannot yet ascertain to which Phoenician structure they originally belonged. The ruins were prominent enough to catch the attention of later Greek sailors to this coast, and they knew the site by the name of Mainake; its Phoenician name is not known to us.

The subsistence economy can be established in some detail from animal and fish bones. From the very beginning, it was well-organized, depending mainly on cattle with some sheep, and fewer pigs, for its meat supplies. As time passed, cattle became ever more important to the point where their bones suggested to the zoologists studying them that beef animals were specially bred by 650 BC. Fish bones were so common that there must have been specialist fishermen supplying the colony; this is perfectly in order, for this stretch of the Mediterranean between southern Spain and northwest Africa has been famous for millennia for its rich fisheries. Industrial activity included copper and iron working, shown by the droplets of metal, slags, and bellow nozzels; purple dye obtained from the murex mollusc, and wheel-made pottery of good quality. Other manufactures might have included linen cloth, oil, wine, and perhaps elaborated fish products.

The colony's graveyards lie nearby, although all the graves discovered so far have been looted, or damaged by agricultural works. On the opposite side of the river, at Cerro del Mar, lies a cemetery of rock-cut tombs of the seventh and sixth centuries; forty-two graves have been found. Just north of the colony is another necropolis at Jardín, with 101 graves of the same type, but including richer cists of dressed stone, and later ones with limestone sarcophagi of the fifth to the fourth century. Only the oldest burials in the cemetery can belong to the settlement at Toscanos, but the later ones show that Phoenician occupation continued in the neighbourhood, now under Carthaginian hegemony, but not at Toscanos (ill. 20).

The area seems to have been empty, or nearly so, when it was chosen for settlement in the eighth century. The scatter of handmade pottery of indigenous types might belong to people who had already lived there before, but one has the impression, from the finds made since 1964, that there was no strong or numerous indigenous element. Nor can we yet talk about a Phoenician hinterland for Toscanos in any detail; it is premature to think it was anything like that known for Greek colonies such as Olbia on the Black Sea, for instance, where farmsteads and ranches formed a densely settled area behind the colony, and provided its foodstuffs or raw materials.

## Other coastal colonies

Seven kilometres down the coast, on the estuary of the little Río Algarrobo, is another cluster of early Phoenician sites. On a low hill 27 m high, sited by the river, is the Morro de Mezquitilla, with a deep stratigraphy and pottery from 800/780 BC to 500 BC. Excavation has not advanced so far as that at Toscanos, so plans of buildings have not yet been defined. On the opposite side of the river lies the colony's cemetery at Trayamar, which has large, fine, stone-built tombs cut into the bedrock, approached by a sloping passage, dated by their contents to between 650 and 600 BC (*ill. 22*). These are purely oriental in style, and are rich graves that belonged to the leading members of the colony, probably from important trading families who headed the firms that were based in Tyre and Sidon (*ills. 23–5*).

A little further eastwards lies a small rocky promontory, rising 45 m above the sea, with the oldest Phoenician settlement yet found. Chorreras is especially interesting because it had only one short phase of settlement, from 800 to 650 BC, and is older than Toscanos; it might also be older than the colony at the Morro de Mezquitilla, and, if so, represent the first Phoenician settlement on this part of the coast, which moved to a better location after a few years.

Still travelling eastwards, one reaches the coastal town of Nerja, but no Phoenician colonies have been discovered there. However, 3 km inland is an important cremation cemetery on a hill at Frigiliana, with grave goods that are Phoenician and Carthaginian in character, including the distinctive Phoenician bronze brooches with double coiled springs, and pottery painted with big concentric circles in red. It dates from the period 600 to 500 BC, and contrasts with the more formally Semitic traditions at Jardín, reflected as much in the type of graves as in the grave goods.

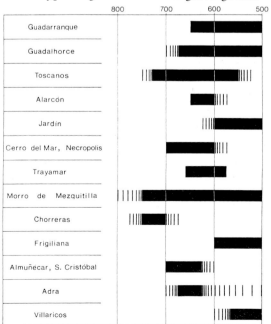

20 The chronological scheme for the main settlements and cemeteries of the western Phoenicians in southern Spain from 800 to 500 BC.

**21, 22 Seventh-century tombs**
(*Above*) Four large vaults cut into the ground among the Phoenician and Carthaginian tombs dug up by Siret at Villaricos (Almeria). (*Left*) Interior of Tomb 37 at Trayamar (Malaga), with some pottery still in place. The neat ashlar masonry is characteristic of the finest Phoenician tombs of the century.

23 (*Below*) A well-preserved incense burner (*Thymaterion*) discovered at Almayate Bajo, Cerro de la Peñón (Malaga). A fine example of Phoenician bronze-working in the seventh century.

**24, 25 Phoenician bronzes** (*Left*) This deer, cast in several sections, may well have been made in Spain, possibly at Cadiz. Work of such quality was still beyond the technical abilities of the Tartessians. Its provenance is simply 'Spain'. (*Above*) Popular items were bronze statuettes, such as these two in the Egyptianizing style, found in the estuary at Punta Umbria (Huelva). They too are Phoenician, but probably made in the eastern Mediterranean in the eighth century.

The neighbouring estuary of the Ríos Seco and Verde repeats the pattern seen before. There is a Phoenician settlement on the site of the castle which dominates modern Almuñécar (ancient Sexi) with some sixth-century pottery, but it is the cemetery on the rocky hillside at the Cerro de San Cristobal that is outstandingly important. A small group of shaft graves cut down to a depth of 4 m into the bedrock is of purely oriental design, and the rich grave furnishings date to the time between 700 and 625 BC. These are tombs of Phoenician colonists, like those at Trayamar, and contain alabaster jars engraved with Egyptian hieroglyphs of the ninth century that once held wine, silver mounted scarab seals, red polished pottery – jugs, lamps and plates – and a piece of Greek protocorinthian pottery datable to 660–650 BC. Not far away is another cemetery at the Puente de Noy where ninety-four rock-cut graves, like the ones at Jardín, have been discovered, but with grave goods from the fifth to the second centuries. A third cemetery might lie across the valley at Velilla, since a gold jewel of the seventh or sixth century came to light there.

The easternmost colony with early Phoenician pottery is Adra, anciently known as Abdera, located like the others on a low hill overlooking a river estuary. Scattered finds of red-polished plates, tripods, storage amphoras and the like come from indigenous settlements of the final Bronze Age in the Levant at Los Saladares, Crevillent in Alicante, and at Vinarragell in Castellón, but these are essentially traded items; there are no Phoenician colonies known farther east than Adra. Later Carthaginian foundations were made at Villaricos (overlooking the Almanzora estuary in Almeria) by 600 to 550 BC, and at about the same time reinforced Ibiza, in the Balearics (*ill. 21*).

Returning to Toscanos, and travelling west past Malaga towards Cadiz, other early Phoenician colonies should be noted at El Villar on the Río Guadalahorce near Malaga airport, with pottery of the seventh to the fifth centuries. In the city of Malaga itself, no early Phoenician colony has been located, and the oldest finds from the castle are of the seventh century. On the Bay of Algeciras where the Río Guadarranque enters is a now-destroyed Phoenician colony on the Cerro del Prado, with plates from the late seventh century. This settlement might be related to the Phoenician sanctuary on the east side of Gibraltar, in Gorham's Cave, with its collection of later seals and engraved rings.

The ability of archaeologists to date the Phoenician sites so accurately has been enhanced by the study of Lindemann-Maas, who showed that the rim on the plates of red-polished pottery becomes wider the more recent the plate is; placing plates in a series, in stratigraphic order, amply confirms this observation. It is convenient because plates are so common that all the Phoenician sites can be linked together and, in addition, the chronology is supported by well-dated pieces of Greek pottery and a few radiocarbon dates. It should be accurate to within half a century at least.

# 4 · The orientalizing period

UNDER THE INFLUENCE of Phoenician ideas spread from the colonies along the south coast after 775 BC, the indigenous Bronze Age societies in the hinterland responded vigorously. This reaction is called orientalizing because of the adoption of eastern Mediterranean fashions, cultural values and technologies, and is characteristic of other Mediterranean societies too; there are orientalizing episodes in Cyprus, Greece and Etruria, where the same stimuli had an equally radical effect. The transformation occurs in Spain between 700 and 550 BC, with an exponential curve of change in the material culture of the indigenous societies. The process of assimilation at first affects only a very few people, and is exclusive in style, but its gathering pace and volume sweep the entire society into the transformation; everywhere it is a rapid process, with speed and intensity of change its essences. In Iberia, the archaeological evidence is unambiguous; the first appearance of writing, the introduction of iron-working, large-scale silver mining, wheel-made pottery, cast bronze figurines, a realistic art style, and a host of new religious cults, all belong to this period.

The objects that are called orientalizing are always sumptuary ones, usually related to personal prestige: weapons, jewels, drinking sets, peculiar ceremonial equipment, extravagant clothes. The people who acquire them are always from rural backgrounds, sometimes from an old-established aristocracy, bent on further gain through monopoly trade with the colonial newcomers, as happened in Etruria. On other occasions it may be a rural elite looking for ways and means to consolidate a shaky pre-eminence. But orientalizing objects did not always reinforce the power of people already established. There is an extra dimension to them. The sudden provision of riches, from a source not controlled by anybody except the Phoenician colonists, would allow newcomers to enter the prestigious cycles of trade and gift exchange from which they had been excluded. The Phoenician merchants not only wanted traditional goods such as bronze and gold, but also those which had been little sought before; silver, dyes, fish, salt, and their provision would not necessarily have been by existing chiefs. The older systems of patronage, based on land, livestock and marriage ties, tended to be stable and exclusive, as in the southwest and the earlier Argaric Bronze Age societies in the southeast. They could be overturned if new sources of prestige goods suddenly appear, since they are outside the immediate control of the ruling elite. The result is a scramble for the new valuables, and the entry of many adventurers, whom we would see as self-made men, bold and avaricious. Their success would incite others to follow, and soon there would be intense competition for Phoenician luxuries. No doubt oil and wine, traded as novelties by the Phoenicians in their own amphoras, played a role as well. These are not edifying motives, and the picture they conjure of greed and ambition bursting out of old restraints is a graceless one; nevertheless, they may be the forces that lie behind the orientalizing period and explain its salient characteristics.

In Spain, these characteristics are the glut of rich materials and their vulgar display; the sharp individuality of grave goods and degrees of wealth; the sudden importance of small regions, perhaps ruled by a single family, which disappear equally rapidly; the opening up of glaring material inequality far greater than anything possible in the final Bronze Age. All of this is characteristic of the Iberian orientalizing period. Much of it is general to the Mediterranean as a whole, a common reaction to the widely admired Phoenician civilization, to Greek artefacts, and styles of trading, but it takes quite particular forms from one region to another. The display of wealth and capital stress that the lesson of primitive capital accumulation was learned early and well; this was a necessary step if other aspects of oriental society were to be copied successfully, particularly urbanism and the political opportunities that went along with it. The mechanism for this was trade with the Phoenician colonists, and its dramatic intensification exactly parallels the orientalizing expansion (*ill. 26*). At present the new consumption patterns are clearest in the

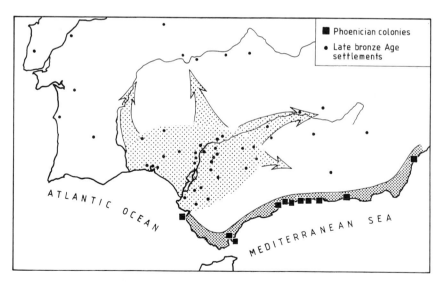

26 The location of the Phoenician colonies established in southern Spain by the eighth century, and the focus of the orientalizing phenomenon in the lower Guadalquivir valley. The black dots indicate important Tartessian sites of this period.

THE ORIENTALIZING PERIOD

southwest and the lower Guadalquivir valley, although extensions can be traced into Extremadura and towards the city of Cástulo (near modern Linares). It appears in a different guise on the Levantine coast, and weakest of all, in Catalonia and southwest France. The success of this cultural assimilation and generation of riches can be gauged by the creative energy of the Iberians, and their projection as far north as Ensérune (southwest France) by 550–500 BC.

## Tartessos: an orientalizing kingdom in the southwest

An unusual dimension to this phenomenon comes down to us from Classical Greek writers who talk of a kingdom called Tartessos, part historical, part legend; their accounts are the oldest to survive. For them it was a friendly monarchy located somewhere in southwest Spain on the shores of the ocean, watered by a great river (the Guadalquivir) where silver abounded: direct contact was probably made in the seventh century, then lost subsequently, never to be recovered. Tartessos was also the setting for the fables of the three-headed man-monster Geryon with his herds of cattle, and of the stories of Habis and Gargoris.

The Classical scholar Rhys Carpenter described the allure of Spain for the Greeks in this way: 'A land of fabulously abundant silver, set at the very end of the entire habitable world . . . made a great appeal to the Greek imagination. . . To the Greeks of the Classical age Tartessos could take on the glitter of a fairy tale because, having once been seen, it could never be revisited.' For us, the medieval tales of the lost land of Prester John, the Christian kingdom of Abyssinia locked in its remote highlands, are similarly flavoured.

The stories about Tartessos are at their clearest in two independent narratives. The first one recounts the arrival of Greeks from Ionia in their fifty-oared ships who reached Tartessos and were befriended by the local king, Arganthonios. This monarch ruled for eighty years and lived until he was 120 years old. The other story is a more detailed one and commonly regarded as being credible. A ship from the island of Samos was captained by a Greek called Kolaios, when it was blown off-course by a tremendous gale. It finally passed out through the Straits of Gibraltar, and shortly reached the shores of Tartessos. At this time, Tartessos was a virgin market, where goods could be traded at a vast profit. Kolaios returned safely home, and dedicated six talents of silver to make a huge bronze cauldron in honour of the goddess Hera, as an offering for his windfall and safe return home to Samos. These are pretty thin details, but we know that the Greek historian Herodotus saw the cauldron for himself, since he described its decoration of jutting griffins' heads on the rim and the three huge statues of kneeling men which supported the vessel. Each was over 3 m high!

53

From these accounts, and scraps of others, it is clear that Tartessos was a mineral emporium rich in silver, which lay beyond the Straits of Gibraltar. The voyage Kolaios made to reach it was about 2300 km each way, and one can hardly imagine that he would reach such a place even in a fierce tempest, or that he would navigate towards it unless he had previous knowledge of its existence and its fabled wealth of silver. Whatever his cargo was, it was traded at great profit. His gift to Hera was the standard one-tenth made after a windfall, and since the talent weighed close to 26 kg, the total cargo of sixty talents weighed around 1560 kg, worth about 300,000 dollars at modern silver prices.

The king Arganthonios was not a single historical individual. The name is a Greek adjective which means, literally 'He of the silver land', an epithet constructed out of the Celtic word for silver (*argant*), and one which referred to any local chieftain in southwest Spain. This would explain how there was an 'Arganthonios' for eighty years with whom the Greeks could deal.

Tartessos itself is a name which may be another Greek word, perhaps a Hellenized version of the name Tertis, which was the ancient name of the river Guadalquivir. Much futile effort has been expended in searching for a city or a state of this name. Modern opinion equates the Greek Tartessos with the late Bronze Age society of southwest Spain, centred in the area between Huelva and Seville, which possessed the vast silver mines of the Río Tinto in its territory. Tartessos is known to us through its distinctive burnished pottery, and the direct contacts this culture had with the Phoenician civilization after 775 BC.

The contacts which Herodotus describes were apparently the first ones between the Greeks and the peoples of the Iberian peninsula; the date of Kolaios's voyage is impossible to pin down very accurately, but it obviously predates the fall of Ionia to the Persians in 540 BC. If eighty

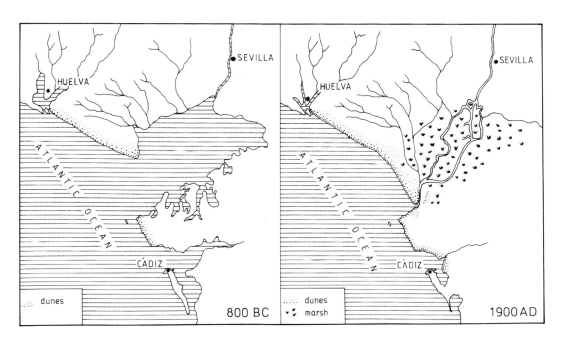

years really was the length of time when direct voyages were made from Greece to Tartessos, this would place Kolaios's trip around 640 BC.

Before leaving these accounts of Tartessos which have kernels of historical events hidden in them, a brief word is in order about the land of Tarshish noted in the Old Testament. References are made on several occasions, notably I Kings X:21, 22, and in II Chronicles IX: 20, 21. These mention a land called Tarshish, a source of gold, silver, ivory, peacocks and apes, which most authorities identify with south India rather than Tartessos in Spain. After all, apes and peacocks were obtainable only in the Orient, and since the ships were described as sailing from the port of Akaba on the Red Sea, they could hardly have voyaged to the west. Whether or not Tartessos was later confused with Tarshish is irrelevant.

## Tartessos: the archaeological testimony

The orientalizing episode becomes accessible to us through the grave goods and rituals discovered in two Andalusian cemeteries, one at La Joya (Huelva) and the other at Setefilla (Seville).

The cemetery at La Joya lies within the modern city of Huelva, on the summit of one of the small, steep hills which form the core of the city, and which once dropped directly to the edge of a lagoon which surrounded them on three sides (*ills. 27, 28*). So far, nineteen tombs have been published, and a few more have been found since 1979. They all lay close to the ground's surface since it had been levelled recently, so we do not know if mounds had once been built over them. The corrosive nature of the subsoil has damaged some objects severely, and the practice of mixing lime in the fill of the grave when it was completed, as part of the funeral ceremony, has added to the chemical destruction.

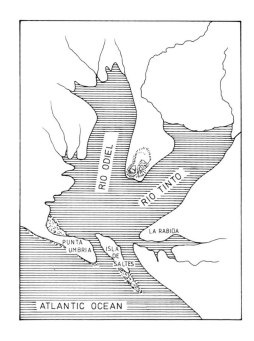

**27, 28 Ancient sites and modern perspectives**
(*Left*) Comparison of the ancient and modern geographies of the lower Guadalquivir estuary, and the area around Cadiz. What is now an extensive marsh was formerly a lagoon, fringed with low hills that made attractive sites for Tartessian villages. (*Right*) A reconstruction of the estuaries of the Ríos Odiel and Tinto around 600 BC, showing how the city of Huelva was originally placed. The steep hills dropped directly into shallow water within the embrace of the estuary. The bronze hoard came from the Río Odiel; the statuettes in ill. 25 offshore from Punta Umbria, and the cemetery of La Joya lay on top of the hill of La Esperanza within Huelva city.

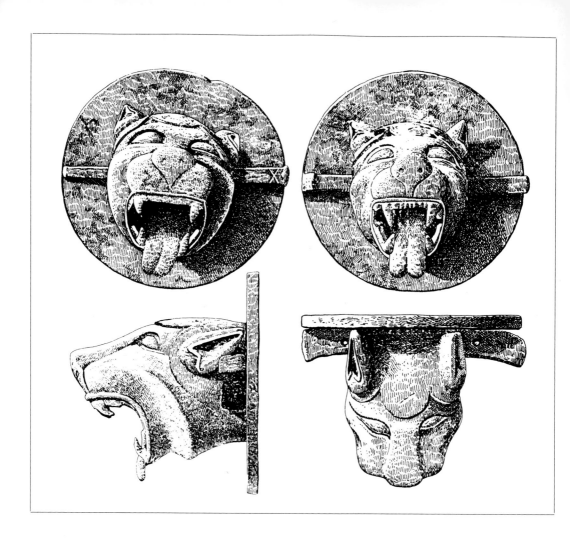

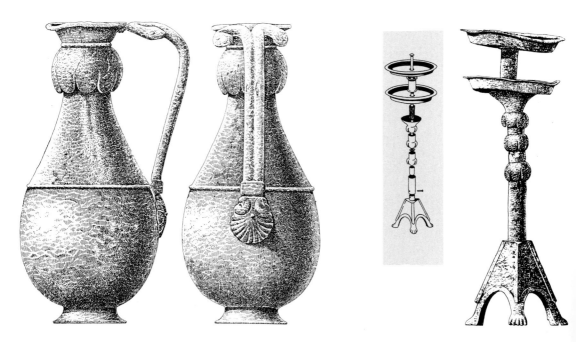

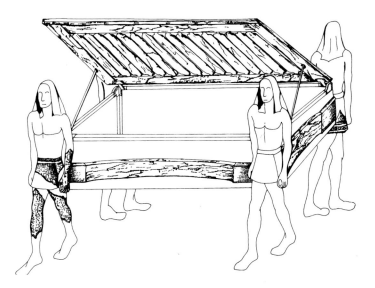

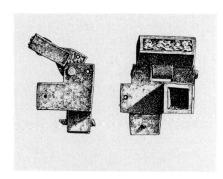

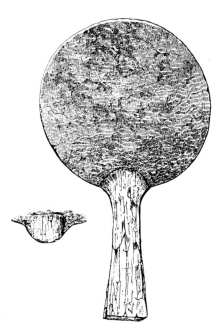

**29–32 Grave goods: Tomb 17, La Joya (Huelva)**
(*Above, left*) Front, side and top views of two bronze
hub caps ornamented with lions' heads, from a light
chariot buried in the tomb; (*below, far left*) two views
of a bronze jug with a serpent-headed handle which
ends in a palmette; (*below, centre*) an incense burner
and an ivory-handled mirror. The manner in which the
incense burner was assembled from ten separate pieces
is illustrated on the left. It and the mirror could have
been manufactured by Phoenician craftsmen in Cadiz
between 650 and 600 BC. (*Above*) An ivory casket of
Phoenician manufacture. The four bearers are in the
Egyptianizing style (like the bronze statuettes in ill.
25). The hinges are cast in solid silver, and shown in
more detail below. The box was probably made in the
east and traded to the Tartessians sometime between
650 and 600 BC.

The most startling feature is the mixed funerary rite, with no two graves alike, and the variation from princely wealth to utter poverty. The richer graves include both cremations and inhumations. The grandest is Tomb 17, with a single adult burial. A chariot of walnut wood, decorated with bronze repoussé sheet work, drawn by a pair of richly caparisoned horses, is the chief piece. It had a draught pole 2.1 m long, fitted with a silver boss, and wheels with lion-headed hubcaps of bronze (*ill. 29*). The position of the finds shows that the chariot was placed intact in the tomb, and was not dismantled to cram into a small space. A wooden quiver sheathed in bronze was probably mounted on the chariot's body. Nearby, personal possessions included an exquisite ivory box with silver hinges (*ill. 32*), a couple of iron knives with silver rivets and ivory handles, and a bronze mirror also with an ivory handle (*ill. 31*). For libations there were three fine bronze vessels: a jug, (*ill. 30*) a large handled dish, and an incense burner (*ill. 31*). A modest selection of handmade pottery included a pair of amphoras.

Tomb 18 was also richly equipped, and although damaged, had similar iron knives, a bronze jug and dish (with handles attached by bronze screws), and a heavy round shield made of leather or wood. There might have been a chariot, too, judging from the scraps of decorated bronze sheeting.

Riches like these are all Phoenician-inspired, if not actually made by Phoenician craftsmen in Cadiz (Gadir). The chariot and casket, especially, show real specialist skills; and importantly, they demonstrate that a market for such sophisticated pieces now existed. The libation vessels are also of excellent quality, entirely Phoenician in design and execution, and were likely to have been made in some workshop in Spain (*ills. 33, 34*). Only the pottery is local, and here the lack of pattern-burnished wares is worthy of note. Many of the items contained in these graves are carved on the grave stelas of the southwest, which at the very least suggests the probability of their contemporaneity. All these tombs date from the period 650–550 BC, marking the climax of the orientalizing phase in the southwest.

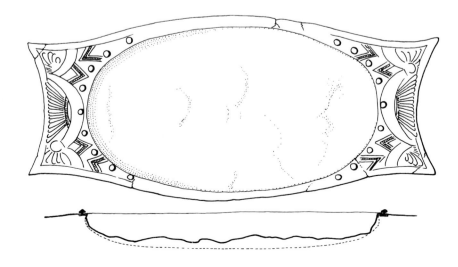

The poorest graves are inhumations without any grave goods whatsoever, and look more like human sacrifices than interments of people who died natural deaths; Spanish archaeologists call them *lapidados*. Tomb 13 held two or three adults, bound tightly in a fetal position, with some large cobbles scattered around the grave, as if they had been used to stone the occupants to death. In another grave like this, the bodies were placed radially around a patch of burned ground. These graves bring to mind four similar ones found, in much clearer circumstances, by the gifted amateur archaeologist, George Bonsor, at the cemetery of El Acebuchal (Seville), also of this period. These were properly built and furnished with rich goods, including ivory palettes and boxes, but the skeletons were positioned as if the person had been flung into the pit alive, and, cowering with hands over face, was pelted to death with stones. The contorted positions do look like death throes. It is a horrid scene. But the trouble with using it to interpret the graves at La Joya is that, there, cobblestones occur naturally in the subsoil, and might have been part of the filling of the grave.

All these rites, possessions and sumptuary fashions show the strength of Phoenician influence at Huelva. The heterogeneous burial customs and wide variety of wealth catch precisely the moment when a few families were actively enriching themselves; La Joya does not show a period after this had happened, of people using 'old' wealth to keep abreast of the fashion, but the appearance of new entrepeneurs. We cannot say if they belonged to the same families as those who erected stone stelas in preceding years, but some scholars argue that they did not. The reason for this thinking is that the mixed grave rites are a sign of a period of experimentation which precedes the adoption of a fixed pattern, a time when 'anything goes, and the richer the better'; once the scramble for influence and riches has settled down, so too does the pattern of fashionable display, with some things becoming accepted as signs of a particular status, and others not. At La Joya, this jockeying for the top social positions would explain the robust individuality of the graves, a trait lacking in the later tombs at Setefilla and Acebuchal.

**33, 34 Grave goods: Tombs 16 and 19, La Joya (Huelva)**
(*Left*) Large serving dish of bronze from Tomb 16. This Phoenician object is unique in Spain. (*Right*) Reconstruction of a Tartessian belt buckle covered with sheets of decorated silver, from Tomb 19.

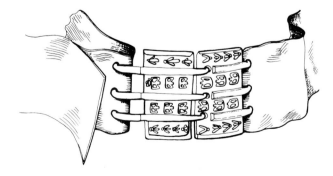

## Carmona and Cástulo

The other orientalizing tombs were discovered in the neighbourhood of Carmona, once an important Tartessian and Carthaginian town, by George Bonsor, working from 1881 to 1927. He found cemeteries of large mounds on the limestone bluffs known as Los Alcores, which overlook the valley of the Río Corbones. He excavated sixty-five of them at Acebuchal, Bencarrón and the Cruz del Negro, and their contents are still among the most important orientalizing and Phoenician 'documents' in the western Mediterranean. Modern work on these cemeteries began in 1973, when Maria Eugenia Aubet returned to the mounds at Setefilla, on the right bank of the Guadalquivir, near the town of Lora del Río. Her studies provide an excellent picture of the late orientalizing period from 650 to 550 BC.

The cemetery at Setefilla includes ten tumuli, of which two were re-excavated in 1973 and 1975. Tumulus A measured 29 m across and 3.2 m high, protecting a big stone vault 10 m in length (*ill. 35*). It was roughly built of unmortared stone, enlarged almost as soon as it was erected, and was looted long ago; it once held a rich burial, perhaps very well-appointed indeed, if it was like the others in the cemetery, or the one from Aliseda (Cáceres). The builders of this tomb were ruthless. They disregarded completely the modest graves already on the site, and slighted many of them, as they scraped up enough soil to form the mound. This violation was intentional, for, inserted within the mound while it was under construction, were four cremations with pottery identical to that in the older cemetery. This also shows that these events took place quickly, within a single generation. Below the mound lay the cemetery of forty-one cremations, of all age groups, including many children, from a population who experienced high natural mortality rates (*ill. 36*). There is little status difference between burials, which were given a large handmade jar to hold clean human bones taken off the pyre, with a few grave goods. Remains of funeral meals were left on some dishes; one held bones from a dolphin. The pottery included pattern burnished wares, some red-polished ceramics, and a few wheel-made vessels painted in black and red stripes.

Tumulus B was different, and contained no burial chamber. In fact, it was designed expressly to cover another small cemetery of thirty-three graves, and did so without disturbing any of them. The grave goods were like those from Tumulus A.

Similar stone vaults were found in mound H in the same cemetery when dug by Bonsor and Thouvenot in 1926–1927, accompanied by rich offerings of bronze, silver, and gold, and decorated ivory plaques, but these were lost in the Civil War. Tumulus G at Acebuchal also had a stone chamber, and even richer grave goods, some of which will be discussed in more detail further on. Professor Aubet's interpretation of

**35, 36 Tumulus A at Setefilla (Seville)**

(*Above*) In this view of the tumulus during its excavation the large stone burial vault is clearly visible in the centre.

(*Right*) The tomb, with its false corridor facing due east, measured 10 by 5.5 m, and its inner chamber 3.5 by 2.2 m. Contemporary with it are four cremation graves (shown as solid circles), inserted in the mound above, which has eight stone stelas on its perimeter. Forty-one graves of the older cremation cemetery are shown as open circles, and the ash-filled pits from the funeral pyres (*ustrina*) are indicated with a diagonal line.

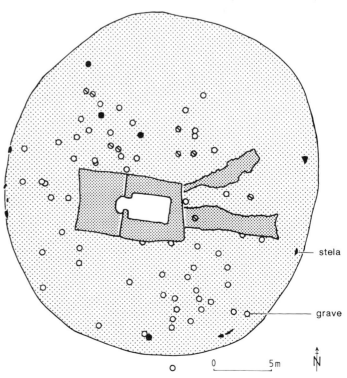

stela

grave

0   5 m

N

**37–39 Grave goods from Aliseda (Cáceres)**

(*Above*) Detail of the decoration on the end plate of the gold belt. The scene of a man fighting a lion rampant is a standard one in Phoenician art. The background is filled in with gold granules soldered on to the back plate, a process known as granulation. (*Below, left*) A gold finger ring with an engraved amethyst seal, of Syrian craftsmanship, depicting a tree of life between rampant griffins, and two seated deities on the sides. (*Below, right*) Gold earring with lotus flowers flanked by hawks, motifs showing obvious Egyptian influences.

these tumuli is convincing: the site begins around 650 BC, with burials belonging to an homogeneous, socially undifferentiated group which practised cremation and buried people individually. Shortly afterwards, there is a crystallization of wealth in the hands of a few people, who can command exceptional tombs for themselves, and perhaps their families too. The differences in the grave rites, although very marked, are due to social distinctions breaking the formerly uniform surface of Tartessian society. Newly wealthy people demanded burials of the most ostentatious sort they could afford, in the new orientalizing style following Phoenician models, copying wealthy tombs like those at Trayamar. This is a social change that occurs relatively late in the lower Guadalquivir, later than Huelva, some time between 650 and 550 BC, and which, once set in train, grew exceptionally quickly. There is no gradual development to chart. It is sudden, gross enrichment that stands forth. The large tombs without vaults at Alcantarilla and Cañada de Ruíz Sánchez near Carmona could be the oldest ones in the series, followed quickly by the chambered mounds at Setefilla A, H, and Acebuchal G.

The settlement associated with the Setefilla cemetery is located on a low acropolis close by, and the first excavation results are exciting. They reveal a strong stone wall of the orientalizing period, which may be the same age as the rich graves. If it is, then the Mesa de Setefilla offers real hope that we can soon study the economic forces behind the orientalizing episode in the Guadalquivir in detail.

Further upriver there are large mounds near the city of Cástulo, along the banks of the river Guadalimar. Tumulus A at Los Higuerones covered a pit grave, lined with stones, and from within the covering mound came a fine bronze incense burner with three animals (possibly lions) on its rim, a perforated bronze cover, a small bronze sphinx, and handles from a large dish. All these are probably of Phoenician manufacture of the seventh century.

The last tomb to consider was found at Aliseda (Cáceres) in 1920. Only recently has the treasure been interpreted correctly as the contents of a tomb, probably a chambered one like those at Setefilla or Acebuchal, and dated around 625 BC. The treasure belonged to a woman, probably a priestess, and all its elements are either of Phoenician manufacture in Spain or imported directly from the Syrian-Phoenician homeland (*ills. 37–39*). The jewels are all gold, and include a diadem, an elaborate belt with sixty-two components, gold bracelets and earrings, a splendid necklace with fifty-seven pieces including sun discs, serpents and the falcon head of Horus. In addition were eight finger rings with seals of amethyst, jasper, cornelian and glass, mostly engraved with Phoenician designs, and nearly 200 gold appliqués from sumptuous clothing. An object evidently imported from the eastern Mediterranean, like the seals, was a green glass bottle decorated with Egyptian hieroglyphs on the shoulder. The treasure was completed with a plain gold bowl, a couple of silver vases, a large silver dish with handles and a bronze mirror. There were also a few sherds of handmade pottery and pieces from two Phoenician amphoras. The jewels form a regalia, suitable for one woman, while the seal rings indicate a priestess rather than just a rich lady. The sculptures of the Dama de Baza and the Dama de Elche both portray women similarly bejewelled and robed, although their date is later, after 400 BC. The bowls and vases were for making libations and burning perfumes, rituals well-attested elsewhere in Spain at this time, and are no ordinary tableware.

All the pieces are the same age; there are no heirlooms. They are most likely to have been made by Phoenician craftsmen in Gadir, a city which was the focus for most of the orientalizing artwork in southern Spain, and also the source for the long-distance imports from the Phoenician homeland.

## Ivories

The better quality grave goods tell us much about the crafts and tastes of the time. One that relied exclusively upon imported raw material was that of ivory-carving, using elephant tusks. This was a skill for which the Canaanites and Phoenicians were renowned in the Orient, and which they practised for a short while in Spain. The Carmona ivories form a group of more than 130 pieces dug up by George Bonsor in the tumuli around Carmona, especially those at the Cruz del Negro, Acebuchal and Alcantarilla. All of them belong to objects from ladies' vanity sets: large combs, cosmetic palettes and scoops, rods to mix ointments, little jars for perfumes, and plaques to fix on small wooden boxes (*ill. 40*). These are purely oriental tastes, as is the practice of elaborate facial make-up for which they cater. The designs on them are so standardized that a pattern book might have been used to copy them out. They are a reduced, coarsened version of older motifs imbued with religious symbolism but which no longer have that, nor even the capacity to narrate a scene; they have become purely static decoration. Favourite themes are lions, sphinxes (once seen as the guardians of the heavenly portals), gazelles, an occasional robed lady and helmeted warrior, and the trite motifs of the lotus bud and flower, palm leaves, and the 'Tree of Life'. So alike are the engravings from Acebuchal and Alcantarilla that they appear to betray the hand of one craftsman, if he can be called that. Other effects were achieved with low-relief carving, and on the best pieces open carving enhanced the contrast within the design. Nine ivories from this workshop have been found at Carthage, and four more combs from Greece, in the temple of Hera on Samos, accurately dated to the years before 630 BC. This is the best fixed point for the entire school, which spanned about a century from 700 to 600 BC. We see a provincial Phoenician workshop here, possibly a peripatetic one; the thematic poverty and limited range of articles are what one would expect at the remotest corner of the

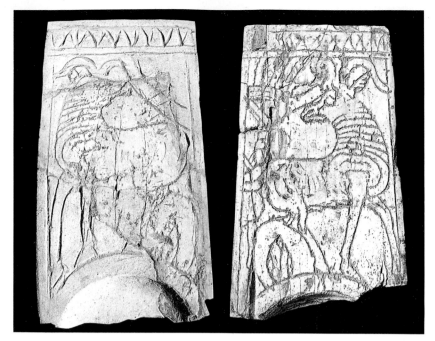

40 Two ivory handles from small 'spoons' found in separate graves at El Acebuchal (Carmona, Seville) in 1891. It is likely that they were used for mixing cosmetic powders or ointments, although they could also have been used in the funeral rites when salt and perfumes were burned. The scenes carved roughly upon them show a horned goat (or ibex) glancing behind itself, with a sacred tree sketched in the background. The crude workmanship is entirely typical of Phoenician ivories from Spain between 700 and 600 BC.

Phoenician world. Indigenous copies of ivory work are lacking, even though the designs were widely copied with real gusto later on. The slovenly engraved ivories from Setefilla H and at Medellín (Badajoz) are the very last of their type, and are dated 600–550 BC. We must not forget that this miniature art was restricted to little items for ladies' dressing tables. Not a single inlay from a piece of furniture, such as the Phoenicians made for their great oriental patrons, has been found in the far west.

## Metalworking

Sheet-metal working skills come to the fore, too; not just the bronze jugs and handled dishes, used as libation sets in richer graves until replaced later on by Greek jugs, but in silver vases and bowls (*see ill. 4*). Gold was also used for large objects like the six matching 'candlesticks' from Lebrija (Seville). These stand 70 cm tall and were fashioned from thin gold sheet, ribbed for strength and beauty. They were intended to stand upon an altar, and perhaps carry small dishes of burning perfumes; they are technically most accomplished, but we cannot say if they were made by Phoenician or indigenous craftsmen.

But it is the gold jewellery that really catches the eye. Orientalizing jewels are quite different from the ones of the final Bronze Age, emphasizing lightness and intricacy. Many have small details repeated scores of times, some beaten from one master-mould, then assembled into big pieces like the articulated belts and diadems from Aliseda, El Carambolo and the Cortijo de Evora. Oriental technology uses filigree, granulation, and gold alloys as solders to attach delicate elements to stronger backing plates or wires. Phoenician taste dominates the choice of designs and symbols. Men fight rampant beasts, fussy geometric ornament covers every surface, and there is a predilection for small chains; also floral elements like those used on the ivories. Indigenous craftsmen became as adept as their Phoenician counterparts, and it is often impossible to separate pieces made by one or the other.

The treasure from the village of El Carambolo, on the outskirts of Seville, is a case in point. It is a golden regalia found hidden in a clay jar, composed of twenty-one pieces of solid 24-karat gold, weighing 2.95 kg. There are 16 rectangular gold plaques from a diadem and belt, 2 deep bracelets, 2 pectorals shaped like ox hides and perforated for suspension, and a necklace with seven gold seals; it had eight, but one was lost long ago (*ills. 41, 42*). The ornament, which unifies the regalia, features rows of capsules and rosettes within raised borders, very glittery and fussy to look at. The necklace is a superior piece, the chain skilfully made to retain its suppleness, and the seals show complicated mounts with *cloisons*, still with traces of green and pink glass inlays. As artwork it is ordinary stuff; but as goldwork, it is an impressive technical accomplishment for its period, around 600 to 550 BC. The massing of simple elements makes one suspect a Phoenician craftsman at work; the necklace is of an altogether higher order of skill, and may well have come from Gadir itself.

Other hoards with orientalizing gold jewels come from the Cortijo de Evora (Cadiz) which had elaborate granulated beads, cornelians, and a splendid articulated diadem. This was built up of small sheet-gold elements, with repeated images of the god Bes on the bottom, set out in gold grains soldered to the background. Chains with the 'knot of Hercules' and negroid faces of the ends hung from each side. Fine jewels have been preserved from Serradilla (Cáceres) and Baião (Portugal).

## Other crafts

Work on other aspects of the orientalizing period goes on apace, and a dozen detailed stratigraphies up to 7 m thick have come from villages of this period. The pottery from such deposits shows that the potter's wheel and well-levigated clays coincide with the first Phoenician contacts, and especially with their better quality pottery. The red-polished Phoenician pottery of the eighth to the sixth centuries was manufactured widely, but with different finishes; indigenous potters developed an entirely new

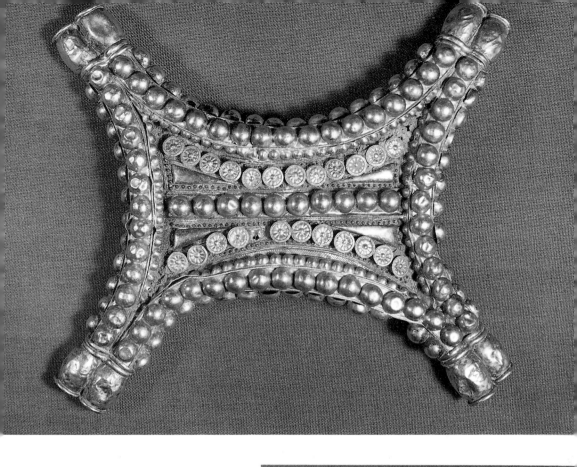

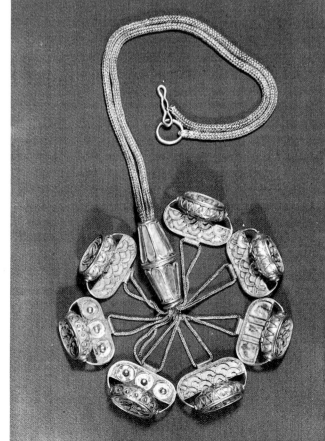

**41, 42 Tartessian treasure**
Examples from the find at El Carambolo.
(*Above*) One of the two gold pectorals.
(*Right*) A necklace of seven gold seals.
The seals originally had green and pink
glass inlays, of which only traces now
remain. The complicated chain and
delicate cloisons on the seals make it likely
that this is a Phoenician piece, perhaps
manufactured in Cadiz.

class of ceramic, one termed 'grey ware'. It is found on all Phoenician sites, and on most orientalizing ones too, and takes its colour from the reducing atmosphere of the kilns in which it was made. It was used for tableware and substantial vessels. Calculations show the steep rise of wheel-made pots, from 2 to 5 per cent before 650 BC to an absolute majority a century later. We do not know yet if the introduction of the potter's wheel provoked a wholesale reorganization of pottery manufacture and distribution, concentrating it in the hands of fewer, and better, specialists, but there is a dramatic increase in the quality of ceramics; the huge production of decorated wares clearly catered to a popular demand. We know that craft specialization is one feature of chiefdoms, and the example of pottery manufacture being raised from the level of a domestic skill to the status of a trade happens elsewhere. We are also on the threshold of being able to analyse physically pottery made in different workshops so that imports and local manufactures can be correctly attributed to their sources, and distributions drawn up. Many centres of production quickly arose, all with a similar repertoire based on Phoenician decorations favouring a red surface, or grouped horizontal bands of red, black, and maroon paint applied with multiple brushes. When new they must have looked bright and cheerful. After 530–500 BC new designs appear.

Older fashions for handmade pottery continued into the sixth century in the Guadalquivir, and their decorated wares can be baroque, with contrasting lustres; they originate in the final Bronze Age around 900 BC. But as luxury tablewares, they are eclipsed by wheel-turned varieties in the 600s, and vanish altogether after 550 BC. It is a pattern over all Andalusia.

Villages provide us with tantalizing glimpses of prosperous societies that are still hidden from our view. There is no site sufficiently widely excavated to provide us with a village plan, or workshop quarters, or even high-class residences. Only at the settlement of El Carambolo can a residential quarter be recognized, with a maze of small rectangular buildings and corridors built cheek-by-jowl, but unskilled excavation spoiled the site. Large stone walls from 700 BC are known at the Cabezo de San Pedro in Huelva, and Tejada la Vieja in the same province; the Mesa de Setefilla is perhaps a little later. Many other sites were terraced and fortified. At Cástulo (the Poblado de la Muela), a chequerboard mosaic floor of small pebbles speaks of some elegance, and it is clear that by the seventh century houses everywhere in Andalusia were substantially built on solid stone foundations. Of the economy we know little, and even less about the impact of new crops and breeds of animals, such as table grapes, olives, and woolly sheep. The one area of wealth production about which we can talk in detail is silver and copper mining, a mainspring of the orientalizing elite's power, which we shall examine in Chapter 11.

# 5 · The Greeks in the far west

THE STORY OF the Greeks in Spain is one of unusual complexity which has changed significantly in the last five years; it is fascinating to see the vindication of extensive excavation programmes come so rapidly. First of all there are the colonies founded by the Greeks themselves, such as Emporion and Rhode in Catalonia, with their own urban identities, Greek cemeteries, and coin issues, so that there can be little doubt about their origins or cultural affiliation. These are so striking that they are handled separately further on. The remaining archaeological sources are less transparent, yet it is they which have provided fresh insights. Let us begin with the archaic Greek finds, not forgetting that it was the Phoenicians who opened up the far west, although the Hellenic contribution was important.

The bulk of the archaeological traces connected with the Greeks are pieces of pottery, a few bits of bronze armour and sculpture, and after 470 BC, silver coins. They are found over the whole of the eastern and southern parts of the peninsula, as far west as Setúbal in Portugal. Except at Emporion and Rhode, the contexts are always Phoenician (and later on, Carthaginian) or indigenous ones. Two routes existed along which Greek manufactures were distributed: one went along the major Mediterranean islands and was directed to the far southwest of Spain, to Tartessos and its silver mines; the other one was much later and reached northeast Spain along the shores of southern France (*ills. 43,44*).

## The southern route

This route is marked by some of the oldest Greek finds anywhere in the central or western Mediterranean, and had the area around Huelva as its target. There is a scatter of fine pottery and bronze objects all along the south coast of Spain as far as Cadiz, then a great concentration in Huelva itself. All of these archaic manufactures fall within the period 800 to 550 BC, peaking sharply between 600 and 550 BC.

The oldest find is a piece of an Attic *krater*, dated between 800 and 760 BC which was found out of context in the city of Huelva. Fine vessels like this were monumental vases, originally intended for aristocratic funerals in Athens, and which, when found outside Greece, are in rich or royal burials. Other imported Greek pottery includes fragments of oil amphoras of the *SOS* type, mostly manufactured between 700 and 600 BC and used for shipping olive oil, either refined or perfumed, all around

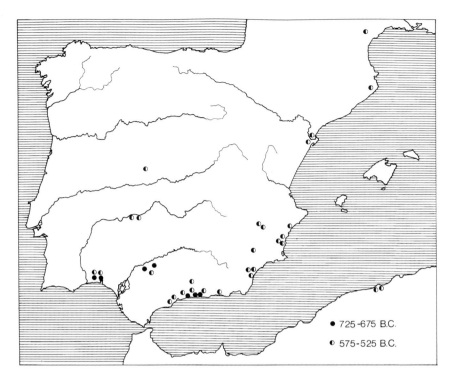

43, 44 **Greek finds in Spain** (*Above*) Map of Greek pottery and other objects older than 525 BC found in Spain. (*Below*) Map of Greek pottery and other objects made between 450 and 350 BC that have been found in Spain.

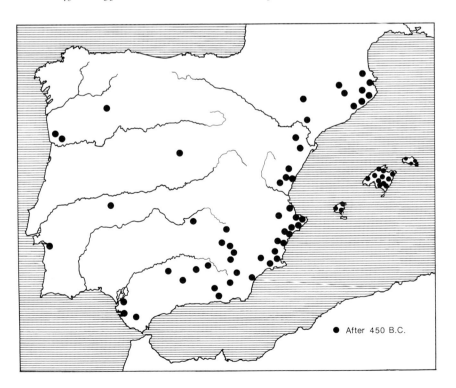

the Mediterranean (*ill. 45*). Other pottery of the same age comes from Corinth and Cyprus, but is uncommon, although it is found from Huelva in the southwest to Almuñécar in the southeast. A few contemporary bronzes include a simple helmet of Corinthian type from the banks of the Río Guadalete at Jerez, with a nasty gash in one side. Opinions differ about the likelihood of its owner being inside the helmet when this damage was inflicted, but concur that the object itself was made around 700 to 680 BC. A later piece is a bronze wine jug of Rhodian type from the orientalizing cemetery at La Joya (Huelva). A notable feature of these goods, other than their marked concentration in and around the city of Huelva, is their relatively high quality, and the fact that many of them come from the eastern Aegean. Their findspots – when they have precisely known ones – are always in Phoenician or orientalizing contexts, and have about them the air of diplomatic presents, or introductory gifts of a rather splendid sort, to smooth out some delicate transactions. No doubt 'gifts softened stones' then, as today.

By 600 BC this trickle of Greek objects swelled into an abundance unequalled anywhere else in Spain. In Huelva, rescue excavations in the modern centre, overlying the ancient foreshore, have recovered more than one-thousand pieces of archaic Greek pottery, nearly all of it closely dated to the half century between 600 and 550 BC. This is a short-lived episode, and the Greek pottery disappears as abruptly in 550 BC as it had appeared fifty years before. These finds are so new as to be still unstudied in full detail, but small wine cups and bowls are the chief forms, manufactured in a wide variety of places in the Aegean. They come from

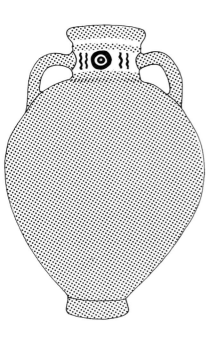

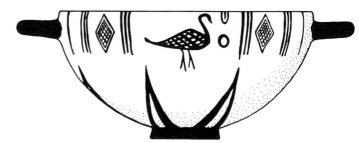

45, 46 Two types of Archaic Greek pottery traded to southwest Spain. (*Left*) An *SOS* amphora of a type made between 720 and 580 BC, and intended to carry olive oil. This had a capacity around 61 to 64 l and weighed about 70 kg when full. (*Right*) A 'bird bowl' of a type made in Rhodes around 650 BC, so-called after the stylized bird painted below the rim. This example is restored from sherds found in the settlement of Guadalahorce (Malaga).

Laconia, Attica, Ionia, Corinth and Rhodes, and two cups at least have neat Greek inscriptions, which appear to be the names of the cups' owners, who could have been Tartessians with Hellenized names. A few transport amphoras from Chios, Corinth and Samos show that wine, and perhaps olive oil, was imported too. The places where these discoveries were made are all indigenous, Tartessian settlements that are either late Bronze Age, or in the succeeding orientalizing phase, and have abundant native pottery, including pattern burnished wares in the lowest layers. One site had so much Greek pottery that the excavator thought he had located a Greek warehouse! These Greek things were certainly appreciated but there is no evidence that they spawned imitations in local pottery or clays, or that any Greek customs of burial, cult, or building were adopted. The archaic Greek presence is marked solely by the pottery, and a few bronzes. This contrasts with the extraordinary impact the Phoenicians had upon the same Tartessian culture, and which enriched itself between 700 and 550 BC. It is a pattern which has the hallmark of directed trade stamped all over it; equally evident is the lack of a Greek intermediary to bring the Hellenic manufactures to Huelva. All these archaic Greek products were traded by Phoenician merchants and middlemen, who had acquired them probably in Sicily or southern Italy, or in the eighth century perhaps even in Cyprus and the Aegean.

Outside the city of Huelva Greek finds are scattered in the graves and commercial emporia of the Phoenicians along the south coast, at places like Toscanos, Guadalahorce and Almuñécar, but always in tiny quantities. Tartessian sites like the village of Cerro Macareno near Seville, and the settlement at Aljaraque opposite Huelva, have the same sort of Greek finds. These include attractive wine cups called 'bird bowls', mostly made in Rhodes in the seventh century (*ill. 46*). East Greek pottery is also reported from new excavations on a 15 ha city site at Torreparedones (Cordoba). The bronzes are mostly chance finds. There is a decorated Corinthian helmet from the Huelva estuary made around 550 BC, a jolly little centaur from Rollos, and a dancing satyr from the Llano de Consolación. An important mixed group of classical Greek statuettes comes from the Balearic Islands, and more will be said about these elsewhere. The only important piece in context is a handle from a bronze wine jug, placed in an Iberian grave at Tútugi (Galera), with native pottery, an Attic black-figure wine cup, two glass paste flasks, and a superb statue of the goddess Astarte. The Greek pieces were made between 550 and 500 BC.

Greek finds on the southern route fall into a very clear pattern; a trickle from 760 to 600 BC, then a glut until 550 BC with an abrupt stop. Not until 420 to 400 BC does Greek pottery or any other Greek manufacture appear again in southern Spain, and when it does, it is no longer in Phoenician or orientalizing settings, but in the graves and villages of the flourishing Iberian culture.

47 Four Greek pots from Emporion (Gerona): on the left is a *pyxis*, a small pot intended to contain medicine; the other three vessels are small perfume jars, made in Corinth (*aryballoi*).

Closely connected with these startling discoveries in Huelva are the legends of Tartessos and the stories passed down from Herodotus. For a long time, these stories were really all the 'facts' that were known about archaic Greek endeavours in Spain, but the trouble with them is that they were already old and uncertain memories by the time Herodotus was able to write them down (around 480 BC). Greek contact with southern Spain was lost by 550 BC, if direct links had ever existed at all. The Greeks claimed it had, and their accounts may yet be proved right.

### The northern route

This route was opened substantially later and clearly bound up with trade based at the colony of Emporion, on the far northeast coast of Spain, in Gerona. The colonies of Emporion and Rhode were daughter settlements sent out by Massiliotes around 575 BC, and from their first establishment were wholly Greek towns in foreign settings; proper colonies, in fact (*ill. 47*). Most of the other places which were believed to be Greek colonies such as Mainake, Abdera, Hemeroskopeion, or Sagunto, have to be excluded, either because they have been dug and shown to be Phoenician (as is the case with Mainake, probably equated with Toscanos in Malaga), or because they seem never to have been real colonies at all, but landmarks for sailors. Hemeroskopeion signifies a day look-out or viewpoint, and was attached to the mighty rock of Calpe; Sagunto has been little excavated, but may surprise us pleasantly, as Huelva has done.

Greek finds on the northern route are very scarce before 550 BC, even in the colonies of Emporion and Rhode themselves. On the island of

Ibiza, the Phoenician and Carthaginian cemetery has a little pottery from Greece before 450 BC, and there is a scatter down the coast towards Valencia. The traditional explanation for this pattern was that the Greeks originally traded directly with Tartessos until the Straits of Gibraltar were shut completely to them by the Phoenicians around 500 BC, and they were forced to develop Ibiza and Emporion as their prime trading bases. This view is no longer adequate.

We have seen that until 450 BC Greek manufactures are scarce throughout eastern and southern Spain, except at Emporion. What follows makes a great contrast. In the succeeding century down to 350 BC, Greek painted and black-gloss pottery is found in unprecedented quantities all over Iberian Spain, and if pottery imports reflect economic conditions in some manner, as they may well do, then this was a period of great prosperity. The larger and finer vessels, especially the *kraters* for mixing wine, were traded to affluent patrons in the south and southeast where many of them finished their service as grave goods for wealthy Iberians in cemeteries such as Toya (with thirteen *kraters*), Tútugi, Castellones de Ceal and Cigarralejo, to mention only a few of the better-known ones (*ills. 48, 49*). Some even reached the coast of Portugal, and were placed in graves in the Lusitanian cemetery of Alcácer do Sal near Setúbal. No doubt these vases had been in use for a generation or more before they were finally buried with their owners, so they do not give very close dates; but they do tell us something about the tastes of the Iberian gentry who seem to have been as fond of strong wine as their Celtic contemporaries in France and Germany. Nearly all this pottery was made in Attica, and although the finest painters of the day are under-represented, there is no doubt that the figured vases made colourful decorations. Work is going ahead to see if a choice of theme can be detected as a preferred one from the scenes painted on the vases; we should not be too surprised if the Herakles legends or some other direct iconography was chosen. Larger volumes of Greek painted and black-gloss pottery reached the northeast coast behind the colonies of Emporion and Rhode. Here people preferred cheaper and simpler pots

48, 49 **Greek decorated pottery** (*Left*) A *krater* for mixing wine found in the Iberian cemetery of Cigarralejo (Mula, Murcia). (*Right*) Two Greek wine cups from the same cemetery.

50 Two Greek wine cups from Ullastret (Gerona), dated to between 375 and 350 BC. Greek pottery like this was so plentiful in the Iberian city that hardly a house lacked it.

than did the southerners; this may reflect the lesser novelty value of Greek vases closer to the distribution centres, and hence their decreasing value, or it may simply be a predilection of the consumers.

Some idea of the volume of Greek pottery imported at this time can be got from Ullastret, the Iberian city just 20 km from Emporion. One-sixth of it has been cleared out, and fragments of over 1900 Greek vessels discovered. We know that Greek wares were imported steadily into this site from its foundation around 535 BC, but they were uncommon until 400 to 375 BC when imports shot up, peaking in the next generation: 80 per cent of the pots arrived between 375 and 350 BC. The picture of a short burst of intense commerce is like that at Huelva two hundred years earlier, and like Huelva, the vast majority is for mixing and drinking wine (*ill. 50*). There are a good number of small bowls for dainty snacks, but they only make up 13 per cent of the total assemblage. So common was Greek pottery in the fourth century at Ullastret that it was in every house in the city, and every Iberian inhabitant could enjoy wine from a Greek cup. If the unexcavated part of Ullastret is equally prolific in finds, then nearly 12,000 Greek pots will eventually be recovered. Granted, much of this was mass-produced for an undiscerning foreign market over 2000 km away from Greece, but it was still decent crockery. This trend towards Aegean imports is generally mirrored elsewhere in eastern and southeastern Spain; most of the pots are for serving and drinking wine.

The volumes of Greek wares uncovered at Ullastret prompted some archaeologists to think of the city as a Greek colony, but this is not widely accepted. In fact, one can see that, located on a small island of dry land with extensive marshes inland and the sea to the east, the Greek colony at Emporion would need a friendly local host to guarantee supplies of food, timber, and raw materials for its daily survival, and the secret of

Ullastret's riches may lie in its privileged role as chief supplier of the Greek colony. No Greek territory (or *chora*) can be satisfactorily defined around Emporion, as can be done at other Greek colonial places such as Massilia, or Olbia on the Black Sea. Ullastret and Emporion undoubtedly had a privileged relationship, and since neither site has modern buildings to encumber its excavation, this could be explored fruitfully in the future.

Smaller settlements also were able to obtain Greek pots, but in nothing like the quantities amassed at Ullastret. The village of La Bastida de les Alcuses (Mogente, Valencia) may be typical of many, and has the advantage of being completely excavated. Among the ruins of 254 rooms hurriedly abandoned by their inhabitants were found thirty-two Greek pots. Most are late in date, but had been in use for at least twenty-five years before the site's destruction by fire around 300 BC. Most other settlements were more modestly equipped than this, or perhaps, since they have been modestly excavated, only small volumes have been recovered.

After 350 BC Greek painted pottery disappears suddenly and completely, to be replaced by black-gloss wares manufactured locally by Greek potters. This is an extremely complicated field, and modern studies by Enric Sanmartí Grego clarify the subject with authority. Workshops were established by 325 BC both in Catalonia (certainly at Rhode, and other sites still undiscovered) and Valencia. They enjoyed an uninterrupted market monopoly over the whole of eastern Spain, from Murcia in the southeast to the river Hérault in Languedoc, which lasted until the Roman conquest in 206 BC. After that, Italian pottery of similar appearance flooded in from Campania and displaced the Greek products. We do not know if the same commerce extended across to Andalusia, because the pottery has not been studied in detail.

## Marketing methods

Who distributed this Greek produce? Almost certainly not the Greeks themselves, but Phoenician and Carthaginian merchants. The early Greek interest in the southwest and its silver mines in the seventh to sixth centuries is substantially later than the Phoenician presence in the area, and while some Greek goods may have been distributed by intrepid adventurers like Kolaios, most were not. The case for direct Greek contact with southwest Spain is still an open one, but the empirical evidence favours the Phoenicians. The picture clears later on. From Galera in southeast Spain comes an Attic bell *krater* made around 440 BC, with an Attic graffito scratched on its foot, which is in turn crossed by a later Punic one. The original Greek mark may have been that of a trader, and in the course of the pot's onward transmission it passed through a Carthaginian dealer's hands and he added his notation to it. Similar cases of Attic pottery from the Punic settlements of Lixus and Kouass in northwest Africa reflect this trading method. But the clearest evidence that Carthaginian traders dealt in Greek manufactures in bulk comes from the shipwreck of El Sec, off the mouth of the harbour of Palma de Mallorca. This ship sank with a mixed cargo of millstones, ingots, bronze kettles, amphoras, and decorated pottery, which dates between 360 and 340 BC. The ceramics include some late Attic red figure wine cups and *kraters*, as well as a number of black gloss vessels. At least forty-one had graffiti or stamps; twenty-six in Greek characters and fifteen bearing Punic graffiti scratched on their surfaces after firing. Among the Greek marks were four indicating the size of consignments (40, 35, 10 pieces of pottery), while all the Punic ones were personal names, such as MLK'BD ('Slave of the King'), MLQRT'BD ('Slave of Melkart'), B'HLM ('Baal is Merciful') and 'BDTNT (Slave of Tanit'). The cargo seems to have been put together at a Punic port with goods of mixed origin, including the Greek ones, and then tramped from one small town to the next. One cannot say if the Galera *krater* and the El Sec wreck are wholly typical of trading patterns in the fifth to the fourth centuries on Spanish coasts, but there is nothing to suggest that Greek traders were busy off Spanish shores trading their merchandise for Iberian produce. Their lack of colonies and trading bases would hinder them seriously. On balance, it looks as if Phoenician and Punic middlemen were the prime distributors of Greek manufactures in south and east Spain from the earliest times to the fourth century. Only in the area immediately around Emporion were Greeks likely to have traded their own products with the Iberians.

## Coins and propaganda

Greeks struck the first coins in Spain at Emporion and Rhode a little after 470 BC, and they remained the sole issuing authorities for the next 240 years. The first ones were small, uninscribed coins with varied designs including a garlanded head, satyr or lion on the obverse, and heads of a ram, cockerel or mounted cavalryman on the reverse. They weighed about 0.6 g, and are able to be dated because of their association with east Greek coins in the treasure from Auriol, near Marseilles. Another hoard was excavated in 1926 in Emporion itself, with the same simple silver coins, but now carrying the legend EM, EMP, or EN for Emporion. These issues may date around 440 BC, since the hoard included coins from Asia Minor and the Aegean islands. These little coins copied the obols of Massilia and are widely distributed in northeast Spain and southwest France. They were in use for the whole of the fourth century and were replaced only when the new drachmas were issued in 290 BC, weighing 4.7 g each. This series copied Carthaginian designs, with the head of Persephone on the obverse and a standing horse on the reverse; the symbolism of these images is unclear. Some numismatists believe that Emporion entered the Carthaginian economic orbit from this time until the end of the century. These fine coins were replaced at the end of the First Punic War in 241 BC by ones bearing an Arethusa head surrounded by three dolphins on the obverse, and a Pegasus on the reverse. Still another major change of type occurred around 220 BC, just before the outbreak of the Second Punic War, when Pegasus was replaced by the odd little figure of Kabeirus, a small man gripping his toes with his hands. With the Roman landing at Emporion in 218 BC the weight of the drachma was reduced to match that of the Roman denarius, and Greek issues of coin ceased altogether in 195 BC. Dating these issues is most difficult, and this outline simply fits the gross changes of coin type into the broad framework of Carthaginian history. Other schemes, no more reliable, can be suggested with the same numismatic evidence.

The uses to which these little silver monies were put may well have been commercial in a broad sense, but their emission is essentially a political act, intended to advertise the town's name, fame, and ardent patriotism of its Greek inhabitants. None of the Phoenician or Punic towns in Iberia, possibly excepting only Ibiza, felt the need to issue coinages until the political upheavals of the Carthaginian conquest under the Barcid family after 237 BC made payments to mercenary soldiers necessary. Until then, they had conducted their commerce ably enough with metal exchanged by weight as bullion, as had been done for the previous two millennia in the Near East and Egypt. Issuing coins had no far-reaching economic importance; no switch to a monetary economy, or new basis of commercial exchange is signalled by the coinages of silver obols and drachmas at Emporion.

To a Greek city, where all the inhabitants were linked together by bonds of religion, tradition, and an intimate political autonomy which was reflected in the pride of citizenship, identity was something to proclaim actively. That is precisely the purpose of these silver coins: to tell neighbours and traders about Emporion, to state its Hellenicity openly and proudly. The actual value of the coins is too small to allow big transactions to be conducted easily, and the lack of either gold for high denominations, or bronze for small change, throughout the entire 240 years of coinages shows that market forces were unimportant. Now, Greek traders were as ravenous for wealth and profit as any others in the ancient world, or Iberia, and did not lag behind the Carthaginians. The mentality of the Classical world in which coins circulated was acquisitive, not productive: people wanted to gain riches, not create capital, and these could be amassed efficiently enough without relying on coinages. Riches were ardently desired to keep up an acceptable life style and so long as that could be upheld, other values were more prominent. Sir Moses Finley put it like this: 'The judgement of antiquity about wealth was fundamentally unequivocal and uncomplicated – wealth was necessary and it was good; it was an absolute requisite for the good life; and on the whole that was all there was to it.'

THE DATE WHEN PHOENICIA finally lost direct contact with her daughter settlements in the west is usually taken as 573 BC, the year when Tyre fell to the Babylonian king Nebuchadnezzar after a siege of thirteen years. Her defeat brought the last of the independent city-states of Phoenicia under the control of the great empires of the time, and afterwards the lead in economic and political matters among the Semitic peoples in the central and western Mediterranean passed to Carthage, to be exercised in ways that are still poorly understood even though their military profiles are dramatic. The last phase of Carthaginian activity in Spain culminates in the brief empire established by Hamilcar in 237 BC and which was destroyed when Cadiz fell to the Romans in 206 BC.

The separation of Carthaginian culture from Phoenician is largely arbitrary, done more for the convenience of the historical framework than any solid archaeological reason. This is why some archaeologists prefer to talk of the 'area of the Straits of Gibraltar' and treat Semitic culture as a continuum, emphasizing the similarities between Spain and Morocco, rather than using Greek historical models as guides. This is a positive view of Carthaginian achievement, if a premature one, and one hopes it will gain force once more is known of the archaeology of Punic Morocoo and, above all, of the city of Cadiz, the key piece in the jigsaw.

## Cadiz and Almuñécar

Punic (i.e. Carthaginian) settlement after 550 BC was restricted to exactly the same coastal strip between Cadiz and Villaricos that was settled by the Phoenicians from the eighth century, and many of the important foundations – like Cadiz and Almuñécar – continued. Only when Carthage launched her conquest of southern Spain after 237 BC, with Cartagena as its capital, does territorial expansion occur. Modern excavations of later Phoenician settlements at the Morro de Mezquitilla and Jardín on the Malaga coast show that commerce continued in a similar way to that established long before at Chorreras and Toscanos. Our slight knowledge of these trading posts grows all the time, and they seem to have had their ups and downs quite as much as modern trading stations do; Jardín faded by 350 BC to be replaced by the foundation at Cerro del Mar a few hundred metres away. This remained prosperous, like the Morro de Mezquitilla, until the change of the era. The more

51 Detail of the face on an anthropomorphic coffin found in the calle Ruíz de Alda in the city of Cadiz. It is of marble, and in the Hellenizing style of the fourth century.

substantial and possibly more successful sites lie below their modern counterparts at Malaga (Malaca), Almuñécar (Sexi) and Adra (Abdera).

The most important of all the Punic cities in the far west was always Cadiz (Gadir), which is all but inaccessible to archaeologists. The Phoenician city lies deep below the Roman and modern ones, and they are all surrounded by the gigantic sixteenth century fortifications which dominate the old city today. Originally Gadir was sited upon a small islet separated from the main island by a narrow channel, which was filled in and built over completely in Roman times, when the city expanded rapidly. Limited excavations show that the ancient nucleus was on this islet, that it was the sole area of habitation, and that its cemetery lay away from it, on the northern shore of the main island. Sanctuaries probably occupied the ends of the two reefs of the westernmost edge of the islet and island, although these have been heavily eroded and quarried for building stone. The maximum extent of the city of Gadir would have been about 1100 by 500 m, only a fraction of what it became under Roman administration. The earliest finds are actually prehistoric pottery and flints dating to the period between 2000 and 1000 BC; and Phoenician material before 600 BC is still unknown.

Gadir kept Phoenician burial customs until a late period, long after other fashions had been taken up in the Carthaginian world. It is likely that this reflects the continuing ties that the city had with the Lebanese coast, and which contributed so powerfully to its Phoenician culture; even Roman writers found this remarkable. Several hundred Phoenician graves were found and excavated from 1887 until the 1930s on the northern edge of the main island. At least 150 were substantial tombs with wooden coffins, intact grave goods, and a quantity of gold jewellery. However, none of the items that would be expected in a Carthaginian cemetery of the fifth to the third centuries were present; no decorated ostrich egg shells, strings of coloured glass beads, or terracotta figurines. There is not even one bronze razor. There are two fine anthropomorphic coffins of a man and a woman, though, of the fourth century and Hellenizing in style (*ill. 51*).

More information on Carthaginian burial customs comes to light from the Puente de Noy in the old city of Almuñécar, where ninety-four graves cover the whole period of Phoenician and Punic occupation. Hope is high that really detailed information on funerary customs, diet, relative wealth and social status in a small Carthaginian town, can be obtained here. This is in great contrast with the excavations carried out by Siret earlier this century at Villaricos (Baria), where over 1500 tombs were cleared out in such poor order that not even a fine Carthaginian scholar like Miriam Astruc could rescue them. They belonged to a substantial town overlooking the delta of the little Almanzora river and contained sumptuary objects, including some large Greek vases. Perhaps the most interesting observation at Villaricos was that an Iberian cemetery coexisted with the Punic ones, and that Punic tombs, including wealthy ones, had been reused for Iberian interments. This is taken to indicate that close ties grew up between the settlers and the Iberians; similar graves were found in Greek contexts at Emporion, so the model of assimilation may be right. Villaricos continued to flourish until 100 BC.

The commercial base of these places continued to be the production of goods long known as Phoenician specialities: silver bullion, dyes for cloth, olive oil for foods and perfumes, wine, salt, fish sauce made from macerating blue fishes in salt, and esparto ropes and cords from the grass that abounded on the hills inland. Dye extraction, at least, is easy to recognize from the huge tips of shells of the *murex trunculus*: some 12,000 molluscs will yield only 1.4 g of Tyrian Purple dye (it gives a deep blue-purple colour)! The silver was certainly mined at the Río Tinto and in the Sierra Morena near Cástulo; many other sites probably remain undiscovered. These were apparently worked by, and controlled through, local Iberian people, who obtained the metal for the Carthaginians and exchanged it for the things they valued; that is, the archaeologically recognizable ones like oil, wine, Greek pottery services and trinkets. Enriched by this commerce, some cities like Cadiz augmented it further by controlling the shipping which traded all the way down the Atlantic coast of Morocco as far south as Mogador, and along both sides of the Mediterranean eastwards from Gibraltar, as far as Ibiza.

## Ibiza (Eivissa) and the Balearics

FOR A MORE rounded picture of Punic archaeology we must turn to the Balearic islands, particularly Ibiza, which has long been known as an important Punic centre.

Ibiza was settled first by Phoenicians, probably from the area around the Straits of Gibraltar, if not from Gadir itself, in the period 700 to 650 BC. This foothold was kept at a modest level until 550 BC, when it was greatly enlarged with settlers sent from Carthage to strengthen the island and take advantage of its resources and strategic position on the shipping lanes in the western Mediterranean. These new archaeological data are unequivocal, and come first from the big cemetery at the Puig des Molins which lies close to the modern city of Ibiza, on the lower slopes (*ill. 52*). The oldest graves were simply cremations in shallow holes, covered by a flat stone. The red-polished pottery from them can be dated closely and confirms the traditional dates that Classical writers gave for the Phoenicians' arrival around 654 to 653 BC. The grave rites are clearly Phoenician, not Punic. Nearby, fragments of storage amphoras of the same age have been discovered at the Punta d'en Tur Esquerrer, which is actually part of the acropolis of Ibiza city, and on a little peninsula called the Mola de Sa Caleta. The early cremations were badly damaged by the later tombs which were larger and dug deeper to form a truly

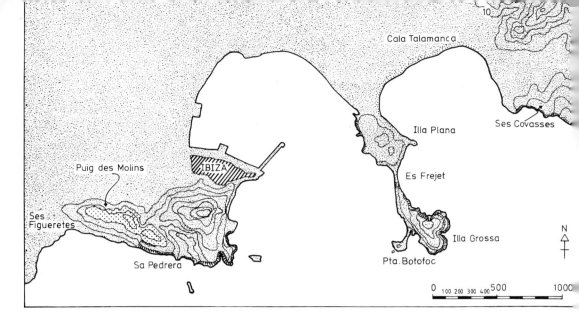

**52–54 Ibiza and the cemetery of Puig des Molins** (*Above*) Plan of the Carthaginian sites in and near the city of Ibiza (Baleares). Ibiza was the main settlement; its cemetery lay on the slopes of the Puig des Molins. Illa Plana had a sanctuary. (*Below, left*) Painted ostrich egg shells were placed in Carthaginian graves at Puig des Molins. They were symbols of immortality and decorated with devices proper to the goddess Tanit; her attributes are shown here and include the crescent, lotus flowers, and rosettes. They were painted in red or reddish purple colours between 450 and 300 BC. (*Below, right*) Glass paste amulets were imported from Egypt and deposited in Carthaginian graves, and are very common in the cemetery of Puig des Molins. The top row includes a falcon-headed figure of Horus, the Eye of Osiris, a falcon, and a figure of Ptah. The middle row has another Eye of Osiris and a crocodile; the bottom row contains a seated figure of Isis, a cow amulet, a cobra, sphinx and a cat. They are all mass-produced articles that were believed to act as magic charms to protect their owners from harm. They date to between 450 and 300 BC.

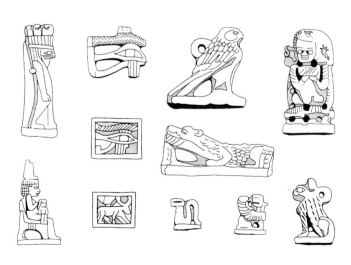

Carthaginian necropolis just like those at Carthage itself, or on Sicily and Sardinia. The graves help to date the colony's consolidation and expansion to the century between 550 and 450 BC, since they have a full range of Punic offerings: amphoras, plates, lamps, small perfume vases, Greek pottery which becomes plentiful after 450 BC, personal charms, jewellery in glass and gold, bronze razors, and rings (*ill. 54*). There are even ostrich egg shells, symbols of immortality, brought over from north Africa (*ill. 53*).

Ibiza had only one urban centre: the city of Ibiza on the acropolis where the modern fortress stands. Using the 2500–3000 Punic tombs at the Puig des Molins, Miguel Tarradell calculated a population of between 600 and 1000 people for the city, that is, the ones wealthy enough to pay for a good tomb in the cemetery. If slaves, workers and other dependants are added on, as they certainly must be, a total population of 3000 could have lived in the town, with a similar number probably employed in the countryside. These figures can be compared with Villaricos which could have had 1500 to 2000, and Cadiz, which was probably several times bigger. Cities like Adra and Almuñécar may also have had more than 1000 inhabitants each; these figures are all estimates, but larger than any that can be defended for the trading stations, which probably had a few scores of staff and craftsmen.

The produce which supported this city was largely agricultural, and traded widely. Fine wool, dyes, salt for preserves, fish sauce, oil, wine and pottery amphoras to pack them in were certainly Ibizan products, since traces have been found on the island of all of them. The entire island was closely settled by the fifth century, with farms and granges identified; they are mostly known from their graveyards, since these were excavated in a search for museum pieces at the beginning of the century. By this time, Ibiza was not a simple way station or port of call, nor a factory site making some fish sauce. It had become a prosperous community, almost a small city-state in its size and extension, trading with Massilia, Emporion and many other ports all the way across to Carthage, Cadiz and Lixus. If we wish to know what a town's territory looked like, or how it organized its immediate hinterland, then the island of Ibiza is a textbook example awaiting study. Prosperity peaked from the fourth to the second centuries, although the exact role that Ibiza played in regional trade is hard to describe. The pattern of Greek pottery imports on the island is identical to that on the Spanish mainland, being commonest between 450 and 350 BC, and comprising Attic products of mediocre quality. Most of them are little perfume vases (*lekythoi*) intended for funerary use, and it is in the graves at the Puig des Molins where they are most often found.

Ibiza was a major commercial competitor in the western Mediterranean and had contacts with Mallorca after 550 BC, which were followed up by 400 BC with Ibizan trading posts along the coast. One of these is being excavated at the Illot de Na Guardis, just offshore from

55 A reconstruction of a Carthaginian forge and workshop for iron found at Na Guardis (Mallorca), with its domed furnace in the centre and the working area behind it. In the foreground are two storerooms for fuel and tools. The complex was built around 200 BC.

Sant Jordi on the south coast of Mallorca. It is nothing less than a Punic factory and trading station, linked closely to Ibiza. On this tiny islet, protected by reefs, are two architectural groups; one with houses, storerooms and dependencies set on the highest part of the islet, with a defensive wall of stone all around them. The other is an iron forge, set apart on account of its combustability and dirt, also surrounded by its own wall (*ill. 55*). On two sides of the islet were wooden piers, now vanished, designed for use when the prevailing wind shifted from one direction to another. That on the north side had shipwrecks off it, one of an Ibizan or Punic vessel which had caught fire and sunk, laden with oil amphoras and Punic pottery made between 150 and 130 BC, and the other one of Roman date, with a cargo of wine and fish sauce coming from Ibiza. Besides these wrecks were many jars and amphoras which had fallen off the pier during loading, or had been thrown there when broken. The other pier lay on the western side. Pottery gives dates between 400 BC and AD 50 for the use of Na Guardis; the forge was built around 200 BC, judging from an amphora sherd embedded in its dome.

This Ibizan trading post was a Punic version of the Phoenician ones set up 400 years before along the Spanish and Moroccan coasts. The emphasis was upon colonization though, establishing a strong commercial interest in an area over which domination could be exercised. That this was so may seem unlikely at first glance, since the station at Na Guardis really is tiny. But there is now coming to light on the island of Mallorca a colonial cycle which was wholly unknown until a few years ago. It parallels that which took place in lower Andalusia in the orientalizing period, as the excavator V. M. Guerrero Ayuso observed. First there are occasional contacts with the Punic world, showing up as chance finds of oil amphoras and pretty goods like Greek and Egyptian bronze statuettes. Nearly all of these things are found in native cultural contexts of the Talayotic (i.e. Balearic) world, which in the sixth century was still bronze-using. This material is heterogeneous in its origins, and for a long time was explained as war booty brought home to Mallorca by successful mercenaries who had fought as slingers for the Carthaginian armies in Sicily. This may be the case with some pieces, but it is more economical, if less historically imaginative, to interpret all the Greek bronzes as a group, pieces traded in the same manner as the Egyptian statuette of Imhotep, as introductory presents in a phase of pre-colonial contact. The Greek bronzes hail from the Peloponnese, Attica, and South Italy.

Once links had been built up, a trading post could be established and more intense exchange of bulkier goods could be undertaken. In this manner Na Guardis grew, and from it were sent out yet other subsidiary way stations to extend its range. They have been found at the Illot d'En Sales, Calviá, Na Galera, and Palma. The iron forge at Na Guardis hints that this metal may have been introduced to the Balearic Islands through Ibizans.

Supporting this fascinating picture of Punic exploitation are the shipwrecks in the area. Off Ibiza at Tagomago is one with a cargo of Punic amphoras of the fifth century; the wreck at El Sec in the harbour at Palma de Mallorca sank around 340 BC and had a varied cargo, including the Greek painted and black-gloss pottery discussed in Chapter 5; and another at Binisafùller (Menorca) which had Ibizan amphoras, among other sorts, dating to 275–250 BC. If all these wrecks were Ibizan vessels, then they reinforce the view of the wide-ranging commerce which we believe made the island so wealthy.

The distribution of the Punic coins minted at Ibiza agrees with this. They were issued in both silver and bronze, and bear unmistakable devices, often a bull on one face and the image of Bes (a grotesque dwarf god of Egyptian origin) on the other. The older ones are anepigraphic. Issues are believed to have begun around 237 BC, at the time of the Barcid conquest of Spain, as with most of the other Punic mints on the mainland. As with so many of these coinages, the simplest question of all, their date, is one of the hardest to answer; Miguel Tarradell favours a date in the late fourth century for their first appearance. These monies were widespread especially along the northeast coast of Spain and the

Balearic Islands; they are common too in North Africa as far west as Lixus on the Atlantic shore, and reflect the range of Ibizan trading interests. The name of the island probably stems from the name 'Bes' on these coins; in Punic it is written as *BSM*, which can be translated as the 'Island of Bes', hence Ibiza.

## Punic cults

Also on Ibiza are Punic sanctuaries and clay sculptures of some interest. No *tophets* (inner part of a shrine to the god Baal) containing child sacrifices, like those at Carthage, Sicily, or Sardinia have been discovered, but in view of the island's intense links with Carthage, such a shrine probably existed. Those that we do know about are less sinister. One lies at the Illa Plana, a headland opposite the city of Ibiza, in an area used also as a cemetery and place for extracting dye from murex shellfish. The cult was celebrated in the open air, for no buildings were detected, and the materials used in the ceremonies were dumped into two deep pits, each 1 m across and 9 m deep. The first had human bones stuffed into it; the other contained amphora sherds, little glass paste vases, Punic coins, pieces of ostrich egg shell, and thirty-five clay statues up to 21 cm tall. They attract attention for their cheerful vulgarity, since most of them are coarsely made except for the prominent male genitalia which are modelled in especial detail. Parallels are known from similar pits excavated at Bithia in Sardinia, and dated to the fourth century. The nature of the cult is unknown, and hard to imagine accurately.

More important that Illa Plana is the cave sanctuary of Es Cuyram at the north end of the island, dedicated to the goddess Tanit. The low entrance leads to a roomy interior with more than 400 sq m of floor space, and excavations, sadly of poor quality, recovered over 600 clay statuettes of the goddess, and a small bronze plaque with two Punic inscriptions written about two centuries apart from each other. The older is dedicated to the god Melkart; the later one to the goddess Tanit by her priest Abdesmun. Other cult objects were a small stone altar and several conical stones. Great interest was aroused by the statuettes, which are attractive sculptures in their own way. One class is of bell-shaped figures between 10 and 20 cm tall representing a robed figure with folded wings and a female head. The other class is of flat figurines of women who carry a torch in the right hand and an offering (or a child) in the left; others are plainer and just depict ladies wearing heavy necklaces. All these figures were originally painted in red or blue, with details picked out in white; a few were gilded. Moulds and broken rejects for the flat figurines were found outside Ibiza city, showing that they were made there and taken to the sanctuary for dedication. These can all be interpreted as popular religious art, not for display, but images of Tanit intended to be offered to the goddess, then left deep in the dark spaces of Es Cuyram.

Other clay sculptures have been found in the cemetery at the Puig des Molins. Varied types break the uniformity noted in the shrine offerings, but almost all of them lack exact contexts, since the graves to which they originally belonged were sacked repeatedly in the Middle Ages. Over 300 are known and can be grouped stylistically in Carthaginian, Greek or Egyptian types; the latter are the rarest. Many seem to be imported from the Aegean, probably passing through Sicily and South Italy on their way to Ibiza. The last sculptural group is the little glass paste masks which copy Carthaginian models and were manufactured on Ibiza. These pieces were to be worn or carried and have grotesque faces, likenesses of devils, Bes, or a satyr. Their function, since they are often found in graves, may be to protect the dead, but they might be linked to initiation rites practised in secret by religious fraternities.

The glass paste and bone amulets imported from Egypt had similar apotropaic functions, and are decidedly common in Punic, specifically Carthaginian, graves (*ill. 54*). Originally they were strung together into necklaces, sometimes all of the same type, others with a medley of deities and charms. Recently a complete one was found at the Puente de Noy: four Horus eyes, eight Ptah figures, pairs of crocodiles, falcons, the goddess Isis, and so on, to a total of twenty-five pieces in all. They are in fact magical charms, part of the subterranean popular religion that existed on the margin of the more respectable official cults based on shrines. Their variety corresponds to the multitude of specific virtues and powers, because each amulet had directed potency related to its shape, and to that alone. By wearing the charms, the powers of the spirits were enlisted: it was a comforting, direct way of drawing divine protection to one.

Finally, for an island so emphatically Carthaginian as Ibiza, the entire absence of gravestones, so frequent in the central Mediterranean, is peculiar. The only one in the far west comes from Villaricos.

## Later Carthaginians on the mainland

Back on the Iberian mainland the picture is quite different from what we have found on Ibiza. Away from the strongly colonized coastal strip, Punic imports into the interior seem to be of little worth. Those that did reach Iberian consumers were all small inconsequential luxuries: glass beads, sealstones, small jewels, or a few amphoras of wine. Only Greek pottery was really abundant between 450 and 200 BC. Punic influence at this time was much more noticeable in the choice of themes elected for Iberian sculpture and art, the custom followed in burials, and the establishment of sanctuaries where offerings of figurines were made. In these things we can appreciate the Semitic influence on the mind and behaviour of the Iberians with clarity, but it is just that; it is cultural assimilation, a deliberate selection of ideas and objects on the part of the native inhabitants, not an occupation, conquest, or absorption by the Carthaginians.

In eastern Spain in the mid-fourth century a wave of destruction of important native settlements has been detected. Many were fortified strongly but still succumbed, and were either left deserted or reoccupied in a poor way afterwards. About the same time were built systems of small forts in the provinces of Jaén and Cordoba, as if to block access into Andalusia from the north, which have long been tagged as 'Hannibal's Towers'. These discoveries have tempted some writers to provide a specific historical explanation, one where the Carthaginians sought to extend their power over the hinterland by subjugating those who resisted them. The motive for this would be the treaty between Rome and Carthage in 348 BC delimiting their respective zones of influence, allowing Carthage to move on to the attack and consolidate her advantage over the Iberians with impunity. Growing Carthaginian influence may be seen in the switch by the Greeks of Emporion to the Punic weight system for their coins around 290 BC. Of course, this picture of increased Carthaginian pressure in the fourth century depends absolutely on precise dating; without close dates there is no history at all, only anecdote.

Historic dates given to the settlements and forts depend on the dates ascribed to the imported Greek pottery; that in turn cannot be dated more accurately than arbitrary intervals of twenty-five to fifty years. These are the dates when the pottery was made, not when it was buried in Spanish soil. Now, it is probably true that the archaeological facts show increased strife among the Iberians after the mid-fourth century, and that some regions, such as Valencia and Alicante, were castigated more than others. This may have been exploited cynically by the Carthaginians for their own ends, to secure more silver, or cheaper mercenaries with whom to fight the Greeks in Sicily. Certainly there were growing inequalities in wealth among the Iberians, which raised tension further. But none of this conjecture authenticates a concerted Carthaginian policy of exploitation, nor links it to the treaty of 348 BC any more than to Philip of Macedon and Alexander the Great's conquests in the east. Even dating the coinages is no more accurate than the painted Greek pottery, and has a large element of guesswork in it, as numismatists recognize.

Where history does come into its own is in the extraordinary story of the final phases of Carthaginian power in Spain, the empire of the Barcid family. It begins with Carthage's defeat in the First Punic War in 241 BC which caused her leaders to send a strong force to conquer southern Spain to make a new base from which to rebuild their country's wealth, and compensate them for the loss of Sardinia and Sicily. The veteran general Hamilcar Barca disembarked with his army at Gadir in 237 BC and began to subdue the coastal peoples, then those living in the middle and upper reaches of the Guadalquivir; resistance increased as he moved inland, but was overcome, and the fate of local leaders who fell into his

56 A general view of the Puerta de Sevilla in the fortifications that protect Carmona (Seville). The core of this gateway has been shown to date from Carthaginian times, specifically the Barcid period. In this picture only Roman and Moorish masonry is visible, since the city was the military stronghold that guarded Seville, and was often updated.

hands was frightful; Indikortes was one, and after torture and blinding he was crucified. A new base was established at Akra Leuke to make Carthaginian operations more effective, but it is not known if it was located inland at Cástulo, on the coast at Alicante, or somewhere altogether different. Hamilcar's end came in the winter of 229 to 228 BC when he was besieging the town of Helike and was surprised by a counterattack of a native king, Orison. He drowned crossing a river as he fled, although his sons Hasdrubal and Hannibal escaped to Akra Leuke.

Hasdrubal succeeded his father-in-law as supreme commander in Spain. He pursued a more conciliatory policy, marrying the daughter of an Iberian king, and became in effect a monarch, largely free from the control of the senate in Carthage. The foundation of Cartago Nova (modern Cartagena) as his capital city in 228 BC was an astute choice too, for the site was a defensible peninsula 35–40 ha in extent, with a superb outer harbour and an inner lagoon. He built a palace there, and a population estimated at between 30,000 and 40,000 people was drawn quickly to it. Hasdrubal was assassinated in public by an Iberian soldier in 221 BC, and his mantle passed immediately to Hannibal. Like Hasdrubal, he had taken a noble Iberian lady as his wife; her name was Himilce, and her home town was Cástulo.

It is with Hannibal that the conquest of the interior reached its greatest extent, with fierce campaigns in the southern Meseta, and into the northern Meseta as far as Salamanca. He may have reached the Ebro valley. In the meantime, the Iberian city of Sagunto on the east coast had placed itself under Roman protection between the years 225 and 220 BC; it was Hannibal's sack of this stronghold, after a nine months' siege with assault towers, battering rams and mines, that provoked the outbreak of the Second Punic War in 218 BC.

For the moment, archaeology has little to add to the historical accounts of this sanguinary undertaking. The capital at Cartago Nova has failed to yield anything noteworthy belonging to this time.

However, at Carmona (ancient Carmo), restoration and limited excavation of the monumental fortification of the Puerta de Sevilla clearly show that the construction is originally Carthaginian, concretely datable to the Barcid period. The central bastion and original axis of this gate follow Hellenistic military plans, then the most advanced of their age. They were modified soon afterwards in the early Roman period, and again by Islamic architects, giving the fortification its present appearance (*ill. 56*). Carmona was the military key to western Andalusia, and close by was fought the battle of Ilipa in 206 BC, lost by the Carthaginians, opening the way to Cadiz's peaceful surrounder to Massinisa in the same year. There may be another Barcid fortification around the city of Carteia, near modern Algeciras.

The other archaeological legacy of the tyranny is the fine silver coinage issued by the Barcids from their capital, and by the Punic cities all along the coast. The coins minted at Cartagena rapidly increased in weight and fineness, and were magnificently engraved by master die-cutters; the portraits are probably those of Hasdrubal and Hamilcar, intended for propaganda purposes, as were the Hellenistic coinages they imitate. They are too large and valuable to be considered payments for mercenaries. Coins for that purpose were struck at Cadiz, which began its minting with them. Lesser issues were made at Malaga, Almuñécar, and Adra, all of silver in small denominations.

57 (*Opposite*) A map of the Iberian peninsula locating the major archaeological sites mentioned in Part II.

# PART II

# THE
# IBERIAN
# ACHIEVEMENT

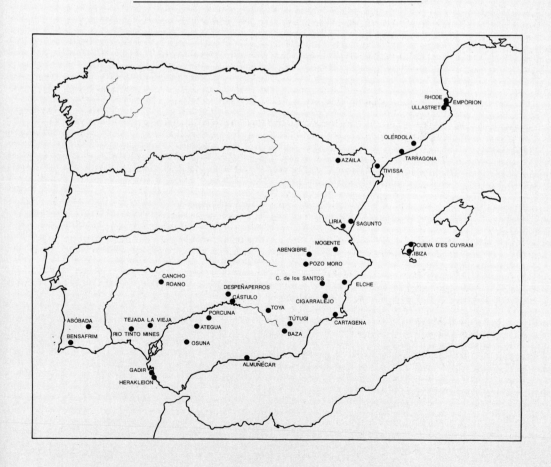

# 7 · The first towns

ANY TRAVELLER visiting eastern or southern Spain at the time of the Roman conquest around 200 BC would have been struck by the number and splendour of its towns. Most writers comment upon them, some with useful detail, others in anecdotes. Furthermore, the urban pattern was spreading deep inland to the Meseta and the Ebro valley. How did such towns come into being? What was their origin and purpose, and how did they affect the society of a previously unurbanized country? Archaeologists trying to explain the origin of urban life in Spain and Portugal have no easy task. Most towns recorded by ancient writers are either unexcavated or hidden beneath modern ones built directly above them, and the two oldest and most interesting ones, Gadir and Emporion, are not necessarily very informative. The former is inaccessible under modern Cadiz, and the latter lies revealed only in its latest stages as a Greek city at the time of the Roman invasion in the second century. So a study of Iberian urbanism, or urbanism in the Iberian peninsula, cannot begin easily from a detailed empirical base, as can a study of other facets of Iberian society and culture. Nor can a contrast be made yet between Phoenician and Greek urbanism.

The issue of urban origins is obviously neither unique nor peculiar to Iberia. Similar structural arrangements appear among cities of widely different cultures, with similar supporting values, as anthropologists have long realized. Historians have been much more reluctant to accept this, but since so many fascinating sites and details will be forever beyond our reach, the only sensible way forward is to extrapolate from modern knowledge about pre-industrial towns in other societies. This is the approach which stresses common factors in social structures, and seeks to find elements held in common; it rejects claims to historical uniqueness. This comparative method has many successes to its credit, among them a clarification of what urbanism is, how, and why, towns were established, even though direct archaeological facts might not be on hand, or available, for many years.

Early cities needed three conditions for their establishment; a favourable 'ecological' base; an advanced technology (relative to the pre-urban forms) in both agricultural and non-agricultural spheres; and a complex social organization – above all, a well-developed power structure. The eminent sociologist, Gideon Sjoberg, who wrote these words, went on to say that 'social power often takes precedence over economic pursuits' and that 'we can find no instance of significant city-

58 A detail of the 'Dama de Baza', representing a bejewelled seated lady, perhaps a goddess, and sculpted about 400–350 BC. Ill. 88 shows a full view from the front.

building through commerce alone'. He thought that too many writers discussed Phoenician cities in the western Mediterranean simply in terms of the commercial or economic factors that could be identified most readily; Sjoberg stressed the element of political power, arguing that this is the key, accounting for the rise and diffusion of urbanism. His main reason for arguing like this was that political power was a prime feature of *all* preindustrial cities, not just some of them, or the most successful ones. Although the city provides the ruling elite with wealth and privileges, its very existence required a well-developed hierarchy of power, an apparatus able to control a hinterland, organize food supplies, or provide a secure defence. Social power was the prime variable for the expansion of cities into previously wholly rural settings, as well as for their decline; or expressed differently, as an urban society strengthened its political control, it could enlarge its economic base as well.

## The first real cities

This is sound enough on a general level, but does it fit the instances of the oldest city foundations in Iberia? Here we have to look at Gadir and Emporion. Gadir, whose Semitic name means fortress or bastion, was probably founded in the eighth century, if not before, from the Phoenician city of Tyre. Its rapid ascent to dominance in the far west – a position, which once attained, it never lost – was likely to be a political decision on the part of the first Phoenician settlers who came to the straits in search of silver and precious commodities as agents of the expanding Assyrian superpower, which annexed their homeland in 671 BC. Assyrian interest in the wealth of the west is discussed in Chapter 11, in conjunction with the Río Tinto silver mines. Some of the Phoenician settlements on the Malaga coast are as old, or older than Gadir on information currently available, although several seem to be outposts or manufacturing establishments (Chorreras or Guadalahorce, for instance) rather than cities. Small trading towns grew a little later at Toscanos and Villaricos.

The other early foundation is Emporion, or 'the market' in Greek, founded around 575 BC from Massilia (modern Marseilles), which itself dates around 600 BC. Greek interests, as the town's name shows, were commercial, but the close ties to Massilia for most of its 380 years of independence shows that something more than simple profit lay behind its foundation; exactly what is not clear. Massilia was already a very large city by 500 BC, similar in scale to the Greek ones in Sicily and southern Italy; the walled area in the mid-second century was over 50 ha, or more than five times that of the Neapolis at Emporion at its greatest extent. A city of this size could well have had its own political reasons for founding and supporting daughter colonies at Rhode and Emporion. The former lay across the bay from Emporion, and was said to be as old, but always eclipsed by, Emporion. Apart from these three cities, there are no other Phoenician or Greek cities to which we can point.

The first cities in Iberia were therefore eastern ones, and systematic institutions in their own right, from the first moment they were set up. They were undoubtedly models for the Iberian peoples to copy, and it must have been clear that one way to do this was to copy certain features of their power structures. Contemporary rural observers would have been fascinated by the wealth, power, and control exercised in Gadir and Emporion. Local elites very quickly set about copying urban forms and social structures for themselves, as the city of Ullastret demonstrates, and the great tower-tombs such as Pozo Moro show that the ideology of power was well-understood and manipulated by 500 BC. It was probably noted as well, that while some commercial organization was required to maintain the political system, it was very dependent on an effective power structure; that is, upon a sustained injection of capital. Anthropologists explain how this can be maintained in cities, and why one needs the other. A compact urban nucleus enables the dominant group to keep in close touch with each other, and the contiguity of religious activities, administration, and favoured residences of the wealthy, all help to create an environment where the city's pre-eminence can be kept going. Around this hub of privileged residents would be a multitude of humbler folk, and slaves, available to serve it and generate its wealth. Their tasks would include manufacturing commodities unavailable elsewhere.

In the case of Gadir, for example, this probably included chariots, fine furniture, ships, wrought ironwork (itself a Phoenician technology newly introduced into Iberia in the eighth century), leatherwork, dyed textiles and perfumes, all of them products of an increasingly complex technology. But the process of manufacture would still be simple since the craftsman would perform most, or all, of the steps from start to finish. Controlling these skilled artisans would give overall control of technological innovation too, and if that was assisted by written record-keeping, an urban elite could rapidly reinforce its authority. Gadir is likely to have had literate people among its population from the earliest times, and there are inscribed objects from the eighth century elsewhere in Andalusia, like the bronze statuette of Astarte from Seville. Documentation for these activities is scattered, but it is one way to explain the presence of chariots, ivory boxes, locally made bronze jugs, or iron knives inlaid in silver like those from La Joya discussed in Chapter 4.

The external aspect of Gadir is not hard to imagine, either, and Isserlin's picture of a Phoenician city in the western Mediterranean should not be too wide of the mark: '(it) would have confronted the beholder with a not very high town wall provided with towers and gates crowned with round topped battlements. Behind it, in the most important urban region, would have been discernible a quarter of high tower-like houses while elsewhere lower dwellings would have prevailed.

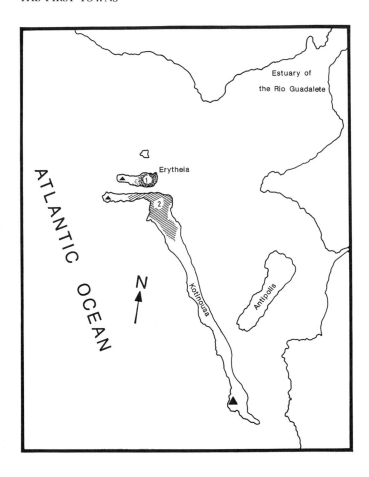

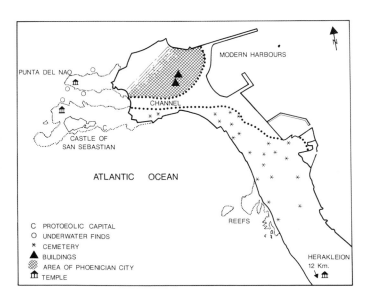

**59 Gadir and Emporion** (*Left*) The Phoenician city of Gadir occupied the strongest part of a small archipelago located off the estuary of the Río Guadalete, as this modern reconstruction shows. Today the three islands are linked together, and to the mainland, by landfills and causeways, and the ancient topography differed substantially from what one can see now. The Temple of Melkart, or Herakleion as the Greeks called it, lay at the southern end of the island of Kotinousa, 12 km from Gadir. *1* urban nucleus; *2* the cemeteries. Triangles indicate sanctuaries. (*Below*) A reconstructed plan of the Phoenician city of Gadir as it would have appeared around 400 to 300 BC. The outline of modern Cadiz is superimposed upon it. Originally there were two islands separated by a narrow marine channel, now completely filled in and built over. Upon the smaller one rose the city of Gadir, and across the channel lay the city's cemeteries, many of which were found during Cadiz's urban renewal between 1885 and 1930. Phoenician temples were probably sited on the westermost promontories of both islands, which are now just submerged reefs. The famous stone capital, sculpted in the Aeolic style, was found near the castle of San Sebastián, and might have belonged to such a building. Phoenician objects have been found underwater at the places marked by circles. (*Right*) Emporion was located on the edge of marshes and lagoons in the sixth century, as this reconstruction shows. The light stipple indicates marshy land; the heavier texture represents dry farmland and woods. The Iberian city of Ullastret, 20 km inland from the Greek colony, had all the advantages of a rich agricultural hinterland denied to the Greeks.

On entering the main gate, the visitor would have passed along a main road for a short distance to an *agora*, near which he could have beheld at least one important temple with probably Egyptianizing architecture, and perhaps other public buildings. Following the main road, or perhaps a parallel, he would have come up to the acropolis where he might, crossing the line of inner defences, have encountered another sanctuary or two. Somewhere on his route (perhaps near the *agora*) he would have noted an inner harbour basin (*cothon*) while in a peripheral region he would have been shown a "tophet". A city of this kind would have been sufficiently *sui generis* to impress the traveller familiar with the normal lay-out of Greek cities as obeying different urbanistic canons . . .' (Isserlin 1973: 144). Most of these details, except the *tophet* with its conspicuous cemetery of sacrificed children, seem plausible for Spain (*ill. 59*).

Understanding the Greek cities is simpler, if only because they are not buried below modern towns. The colonies of Emporion and Rhode were sited next to extensive marshes and lagoons, several kilometres from any decent farmland. The choice of location is hard to explain; the shortage of arable land, the relatively meagre copper and lead resources in the

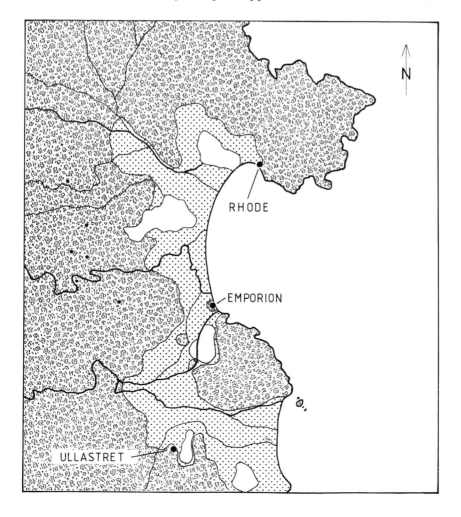

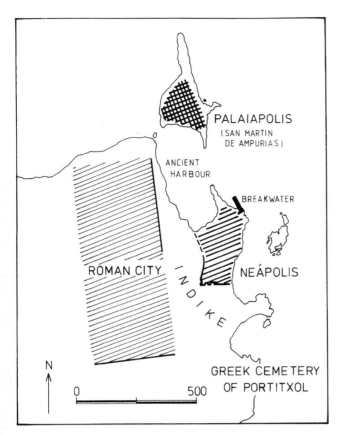

60, 61 **Emporion** (*Left*) A simplified plan of the Greek colony, showing the three separate stages through which the town grew, beginning with the Palaiapolis around 575 BC. The ancient harbour is now silted up and has become farmland. (*Right*) A general view of the Palaiapolis of the Greek colony of Emporion (at Ampurias, Gerona), looking northeast across the bay towards Rosas. The medieval settlement of Sant Marti d'Empuries was no larger than the original Greek colony.

surrounding hills, and the lack of routes that lead into interior Spain make one look elsewhere. But the Bay of Rosas on which they look is an exceptionally fine anchorage when the wind impedes sailors travelling eastwards to Massilia, and shields them even in heavy gales. Security may have been another element in the choice. All in all, these would not have been *prima facie* reasons for a colonial foundation; more likely there were compelling political demands in Massilia which dictated the establishment of these lagoon-side sites.

At Emporion there are the three successive and adjacent cities (*ill. 60*). The oldest is the Palaiapolis, located on a rocky islet, barely large enough for the six small blocks of houses and the church which now occupy it (*ill. 61*). It was the site of a small Bronze Age village before the Greeks settled there around 575 BC, and almost at once they built a stout wall of dressed sandstone blocks. Before 500 BC they had outgrown this place and established a larger town on the mainland with regularly laid-out streets and an *agora* just to the south. By 400 to 350 BC it was surrounded by a rough cyclopean stone wall, that was refurbished in 237 against the Carthaginian general Hamilcar, Hannibal's father. Later remodelling

enlarged the temple precinct and the *agora*. The excavated plan of the
Neapolis, as this later Greek town is now known, shows a Hellenistic city
of the second century. Classical writers tell us that, by then, it was closed
in by a much larger native Iberian town of the Indikete people, to the
extent that the Greek city was referred to by some archaeologists as little
more than a '*barrio*', or specialized quarter, of this larger urban unit. It
too was surrounded by a cyclopean wall. Strabo and Livy described this
city on the eve of Cato's arrival in 195 BC as a '*dipolis*', a double city
divided by a wall separating the Greek quarter from the Iberian one
outside it. The troubled times during the Second Punic War required a
constant armed guard at the gate and on the walls, but this was a quite
exceptional defensive measure. Lacking really fine public buildings,
sculptures, sporting a mean little market-place, and crudely made town
walls, Emporion gives an impression of rusticity, almost barbarism. The
finest extant Greek building is, ironically, the *malecón* or stone
breakwater for the harbour. No doubt mercantile interests dominated
many other matters, but the city was no more imposing than the nearby
Iberian one of Ullastret.

Emporion has cemeteries entirely Greek in character. The oldest lies at Portitxol, 1 km down the coast from the Palaiopolis, and contains Greek imported grave goods exclusively of the sixth century. Later cemeteries belonging to the Neapolis were made near the northeast wall at Martí and Bonjoan; the last Greek burials were on a hill at Las Corts. These cemeteries gave the richest collection of Greek pottery yet found in Spain, and it is noticeable that no similar cemeteries have come to light near any of the other sites mentioned as possible Greek colonies like Sagunto or Hemeroskopeion (Calpe).

## Cities of the Iberians

Twenty kilometres from Emporion lies the city of Ullastret, without doubt the finest Iberian town yet investigated in Spain, which provides a unique chance to see how an urban design was accepted and copied by a previously rural society. The entire area around Emporion (the Ampurdán) shared a homogeneous material culture in the final Bronze Age, typical of the last phase of the Urnfields, which spread over the whole region from the Ebro river to southwest France. Greek colonists at Rhode and Emporion around 575 BC made an immediate impact on this region, most clearly on the two settlements at Ullastret. Both were on hills formerly surrounded by lagoons, now drained, but which still flood occasionally today to restore the old topography. The smaller and lower site is called Illa d'En Reixach, and rises a mere 6 m above the lagoon. This began life around 600 BC as a dispersed settlement of several hectares, with handmade Urnfield pottery, stratified with sherds of an early Phoenician amphora. Around 575 BC Greek pottery – Ionian painted wine cups, and wheel-made 'grey ware' – appears, along with the first pieces of iron in Catalonia. This material is exactly contemporary with the oldest pottery on the Palaiopolis of Emporion. Then a sudden change occurs around 550 BC; we find masses of wheel-made pottery of Iberian styles already familiar in southeast Spain, decorated with painted bands and circles, making up to 50 per cent of the total assemblage, and clearly from different workshops. At the same time rectangular stone houses copying Greek ones are built; these Iberian features are repeated equally abruptly on at least eight other sites in the immediate area around Emporion.

Comparable events took place on the larger hilltop of San Andreu, only 900 m from the Illa d'En Reixach; but this settlement grew rapidly into a walled city in less than three generations (*ill. 62*). There is the same glut of Iberian pottery beginning about 550 BC, followed very closely by imported Greek pottery from Attica, dated to 535–530 BC. Greek pottery becomes so common that by 375 BC it is found in practically every house in the city. The fact that the oldest Ionian Greek pottery occurs on the smaller site, and the later Attic wares at San Andreu, shows that the older

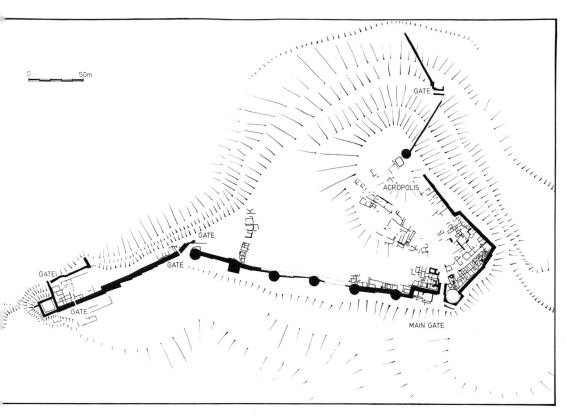

62 The Iberian city of Ullastret (Gerona) flourished from 535 to 200 BC, and has been extensively excavated. This plan shows the exceptional strength of its fortifications and the orderly arrangement of streets and houses on Greek lines. The major square probably lies in the centre of the town, and has not been excavated. The area of the acropolis has been damaged by the medieval castle, although enough remains to suggest that it was the site of important sanctuaries.

settlement was superseded swiftly by San Andreu once it was safely established.

Ullastret city is on a scarped hilltop rising 30 m above the plain, occupying an area of about 11 ha. At least 880 m of city wall have been uncovered, reinforced with seven solid round towers at regular intervals. This is pierced by seven gateways leading into a densely inhabited city, divided into blocks by paved roads. Some lead to the acropolis with its own inner series of walls and small temples; others lead to the porticoed market-place. The date of the walls is now firmly established at around 500 BC, if not a few years before; they are at least as old, or older, than the wall around the Neapolis of Emporion (*ill. 63*). Standing 4 m tall today, with varied styles of masonry caused by rebuildings, they were nevertheless carried still higher by extra courses of mud-brick and timber frames. No other sites in Catalonia show such precocious urbanism, and there must have been a close bond between Emporion and Ullastret to account for it. Only in the fourth century do other Iberian sites in the region acquire fortifications, coinciding with a later phase of Iberian

63 A view along the walls of Ullastret (Gerona). The round towers were built before 500 BC and later joined together by stretches of indented wall. Several phases of rebuilding can be detected.

prosperity and expansion, visible too in the changed patterns of pottery imports from Greece. The end of the city came around 200 BC, when it was destroyed and never again reoccupied.

For a city like Ullastret to develop so rapidly and absorb Greek styles and urban institutions so profoundly indicates a really determined political effort on the part of local leaders, at some time in the later sixth century. It is so thoroughly urban that for a time it was believed to be a Greek city, although this is now discounted. The upper class who controlled and organized the city must have benefited greatly from it, and we must look forward to the discovery of the cemeteries that belong to them for more information. Future assessments of the relationship between Emporion and Ullastret will also have to account for the large town, belonging to the Indiketes as did Ullastret, adjoining the Neapolis, as well as the culturally homogeneous hinterland of the Ampurdán. Future work will revolutionize our understanding of these fascainting cities.

Several other imposing walled settlements are known from Catalonia, among them Tivissa and Tarragona. Tivissa overlooks the Ebro river at the point where it crosses the coastal plain, and therefore commands an entrance to the interior. It covers 4 ha, has a powerfully defended gateway closely modelled on Greek plans of the fourth century, and two fine hoards of silver vessels of the third century. It could well be urbanized like Ullastret. Tarragona is a puzzle. The 30 ha enclosed by the cyclopean wall, built to a massive 8 m thickness, are among the biggest in Iberia. Recent finds indicate that this city wall was probably built just after 217 BC by the Roman adminstration for its main headquarters during the Second Punic War, and that local Iberian labourers and masons were drafted in to build the fortress for the Romans, but in their own style. So Tarragona is to be interpreted as a Roman, not an Iberian, city. This leaves the last great town, Saguntum (Sagunto), just north of Valencia. Despite its historic importance, and its siege and capture in 219 BC by Hannibal, it has been impossible to do much archaeological work on the Iberian remains, since they are either beneath the modern town or smashed up by the enormous fortifications on the acropolis. Saguntum's position is impossible to improve strategically; it is an isolated rock lying athwart the coastal plain at its narrowest point guarding the only easy access to interior Spain through the mountains behind it. Ancient authors talk about it in a manner which implies it was as rich and important as Emporion, but all that has been identified is the base of a stone temple, perhaps the one dedicated to Artemis.

The cities in the Ampurdán fulfil amply the three conditions that Sjoberg listed as essentials for urbanization. As late as 600 BC there is still an undifferentiated, poor, bronze-using society; into this comes the new technology of ironworking, novelties like painted pottery, and wine jars, all there by 575 BC. Within another twenty-five years wheel-made pottery is locally manufactured on a large scale, with ordinary housing following new patterns too. By 525 to 500 BC the ramparts at Ullastret are going up, and this while there were still settlements in the area making handmade pottery wholly in the prehistoric manner. The sequence shows that privileged access to a new range of prestige goods, and a new technology, lead to enhanced status with all its advantages, and that is then reinforced by the privileged group making the attempt, here successfully, to consolidate their power through the establishment of a city on the Greek model. Its source of power may lie in the control of the vital foodstuffs that Emporion need for its survival. A second burst in activity occurs between 425 and 350 BC, when many Iberian sites in Catalonia expand,

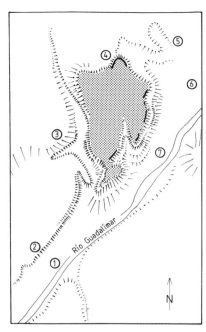

64 (*Left*) The Iberian city of Cástulo (Jaén) is shown as the shaded area, which occupies 40 ha. The dark lines mark the surviving city walls of Roman or later date which follow the original defences. The cemeteries of the prehistoric city are numbered from 1 to 6; 7 marks the site of the orientalizing settlement of Baños de la Muela. *1* Caldona; *3* Estacar de Robarinas; *3* Los Patos; *4* Puerta Norte; *5* Casa Blanca; *6* Baños de la Muela.

65 (*Right*) A plan of the Tartessian and Iberian city of Tejada la Vieja (Huelva), anciently known as Ituci. It was occupied from 900 to 300 BC.

build walls, and set up fresh settlements, usually well fortified. This prosperity coincides with the appearance on all sites of Punic and Massiliote amphoras in large numbers.

## The politics behind urbanism

Now, this account has mentioned the political nature of colonial foundations, because it is frequently ignored. From another view, these cities are emporia, or gateway, communities, placed on trade routes once long-distance exchange began to be profitable. Such places operated with many specialists, principally middlemen and artisans, rather than producers of bulk commodities or foodstuffs. They concentrated upon wholesaling rather than retailing, and hence their importance as market-places, and their well-known political sensitivity. Their very names bear this out – Gadir is born as a fortress; Emporion as a market. But the *Iberian* cities in Catalonia, or elsewhere as far as we can tell, had a different function.

A second point arises from this angle of thought, which is the uneven spread of the urban model in the peninsula. While we can see precocious imitation in Catalonia of a Greek type, and in western Andalusia of what may be a Phoenician one, the same cannot be said for the Ebro valley, where settlements large enough to be called towns are unknown before the late third century, if then. Large areas of the east and southeast of the country were deeply imbued with Iberian cultural styles of pottery and metalwork, yet had few urban nuclei of their own. This is an ancient and significant irregularity that will become increasingly important in future assessments of the Iberian achievement. It is a contrast which has all the marks of a political choice; there may be structural factors in some

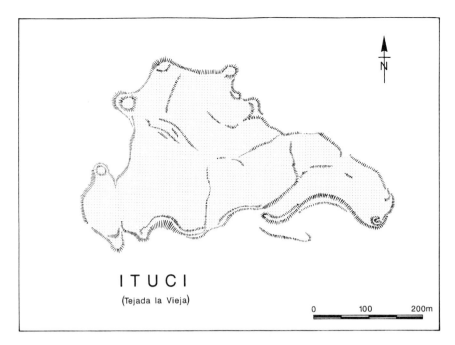

I T U C I

(Tejada la Vieja)

0        100        200m

indigenous societies which made urban life uncongenial, or a recognition that its benefits would be concentrated in a few hands and hence a threat to existing elites. How these choices were made, and for what reasons, are questions we cannot answer for the moment.

The population centres in western Andalusia were called cities by ancient writers, even though they probably had a different aspect from the Graeco-Roman ones with which they were familiar. They are large, well defended, cleverly located settlements, well over forty in all, ranging in size from 3 to 45 ha. Some issued coinages in the second century, and so have a name known to us; others became important Roman cities, such as Ategua, Cástulo, Osuna and Carmona. Intensive excavation on any of them has scarcely begun, and that which has is recent, with provisional results. The cases of Cástulo, near the modern city of Linares (Jaén), and Tejada la Vieja (Huelva) on the route to the silver mines of the Río Tinto, are probably typical of many others, like Torreparedones (Cordoba), now being tested archaeologically for the first time.

The first of these two towns owes its fortune to a strategic position upon important trade routes leading to the silver mines in its vicinity. Cástulo occupies a flat-topped hill with scarped sides, overlooking the Guadalimar river; in Carthaginian and Roman times a circuit wall protected most of it, enclosing at least 40 ha (*ill. 64*). But what of its origins, its prehistoric and Iberian roots? The pattern of scattered cemeteries all around it looks like that common in other regions upon the threshold of urbanization; Etruria, for instance, in the period from 900 to 700 BC, when different communities lived close by, perhaps even in separate settlements, around the same hill. Until a detailed survey shows the exact extent and density of occupation at a particular period, it is

impossible to say how large or rich a settlement was, much less if it was urban. This applies, too, in the instance of Tejada la Vieja, only a little smaller than Cástulo and extensively walled around much of its perimeter after 700 BC (*ill. 65*). This defence was refurbished at intervals until the fourth century, and reached a length of over 1.6 km, bastioned at the angles and ringed outside with a 5 m wide ditch. The excavators considered it to be a native Bronze Age settlement which became a Phoenician town about 650 BC, and a century later adopted Iberian pottery and material culture. The town was abandoned in 300 BC, and relocated at Tejada la Nueva, 5 km to the north, perhaps on a Carthaginian initiative; its coins bear the name Ituci. A better interpretation would be to see this town as another Ullastret, an example of thorough acculturation to Phoenician patterns in the seventh century on the part of the local inhabitants, who later accepted new pottery fashions originating farther east; it is improbable that it was a Phoenician town any more than Ullastret was a Greek one.

Size is not really an accurate index of urban importance, any more than is the scale of the defences. Contemporary building styles also vary widely. There is cyclopean walling at Tarragona, regular squared blocks of masonry at Ibros (Jáen), and pseudo-polygonal building with closely fitted, irregular blocks at Olérdola (Tarragona) (*ill. 66*). At the moment, we have to accept the insistence of Classical writers that many of these places were indeed Iberian towns, and the emphasis upon their ancient commitment to urban values should alert us that many more fine cities like Ullastret await discovery in the south.

Support for this idea comes from the territorial characteristics of these towns. They form central places, the foci of an area, populated with lesser settlements that depend upon them for administrative and other services. These territories organize the landscape in a pattern, with the towns forming the nodes of dense networks of forts, farming villages, specialized mining or fishing places, and perhaps small markets. They are drawn together under a single jurisdiction, based on the town, which provides their essential political support. These modules are the same as autonomous city-states. A convincing pattern can be made of the Etruscan cities in Italy, each at the centre of their small domains, or of Mycenaean and Cretan palaces in Bronze Age Greece. This common pattern belongs to free political units, based on towns (Etruria) or palaces (Bronze Age Greece) that had equivalents in the Phoenician city states of the Levant and the Greek ones in the Classical period. It seems very probable that similar territories can be identified for these Iberian cities, as it has been for the Romanized ones in the Ebro valley after 200 BC. The

66 A tower in the fortifications of Olérdola (Tarragona). The irregular, polygonal masonry in the lower courses is Iberian, as are long stretches of the circuit wall on the site. The battlements are medieval additions.

political models were close at hand for imitation, and a wide variety of oligarchies, tyrannies, monopolies and monarchies could be found within the Phoenician and Greek world in the central Mediterranean. We know that Iberian soldiers were fighting as mercenaries in Sicily as early as the battle of Himera (480 BC), and so had a choice opportunity for close observation. For all these reasons, the Iberian towns are likely to have been autonomous and independent, akin in form and operation to other city-states. Whether or not they were able to combine into larger state systems, as opposed to temporary confederacies, is nearly impossible to say. It seems too much to expect of even the richest Iberian cities, but from their number, size, and distribution, they conform to the broad pattern that can be seen in Etruria. Doubtless there was a great variety of institutional experiment in these towns, and one should not expect one system to be dominant.

# 8 · Art and the ideology of power

ARCHITECTURE AND STONE SCULPTURE figure prominently in the repertoire of Iberian culture, and are usually discussed in terms of their artistic quality, relationship to superior Greek models, and their date. Selective judgments still abound, but can largely be set aside thanks to the discoveries by Martín Almagro Gorbea at the site of Pozo Moro, and widely publicized in the past decade. This is the first competent excavation to recover the *context* in which the pieces of sculpture were originally displayed, and a complete reassessment of Iberian stone carving is now under-way. Sculpture had a specific position on monuments, and had a clear development in relation to their architecture. Most carvings and figures were for display on grandiose tombs, or atop freestanding stone pillars, and can be interpreted as part of a coherent ideology.

The tomb of Pozo Moro lies on the open plain near Chinchilla de Monte Aragón, far from any major settlement. This part of Albacete is flat, arid, and desolate, important solely on account of the ancient routes from the Mediterranean to the southern Meseta and the silver mines farther inland. The monument was built as a tower tomb at least 5 m tall and 3.65 m square at the base. It may have been much taller than this if it had once been surmounted by a pyramidal ornament like the Phoenician ones in Syria (*ill. 67*). The entire structure was of dressed limestone blocks, worked on the spot, as the masons' chippings show. Lead cramps held the stones together, and some had mason's marks cut on them. The base was constructed of three large steps, surmounted by a tower which carried friezes, sculpted in low relief, on all four sides. This was capped with elaborate cornices and cable mouldings. A filling of smaller stones and clay consolidated the tower, but it is uncertain if there was ever an interior room or burial chamber within it. Around the outside was laid a neat pavement of small pebbles, contained by a low mud-brick wall, and that had a narrower pebble path running outside it.

The tomb collapsed only a few decades after it had been built, partly due to the lack of foundations (a sign of the builders' inexperience), and partly because the weight of the infilling was too much for the structure to support. Around and above its ruins, from 450 BC onwards, a rich Iberian cemetery was established, respecting the sanctity of the site and reusing many stones from the great tomb.

The only grave goods came from an ash-filled *bustum* directly below the base of the tower, marking the place where the body of the tomb's owner was cremated. Although the fierce heat had left only minute traces of calcined bone, iron, bronze, silver and gold, there were three Greek objects still identifiable: a wine cup painted with a young male dancer twirling on one foot; a small perfume jar; and a little bronze sculpture from the handle of a wine jug. The pottery is Attic, and closely datable to within a few years of 500 BC. The sculpture is that of a naked youth, grasping two lions by their tails; it is the familiar theme of the 'Lord of the Animals', and one often found in later Iberian art. No other artefacts could be associated with the monument, nor is it known if there was ever a rich cache of offerings made elsewhere within the tomb. These artefacts form a coherent group that was likely to have been used to pour libations in the funerary rites while the body was being burned in the funeral pyre. Similar combinations of wine cups and jars are found in older graves copying Phoenician fashions in western Iberia.

The sculpture consists of four massive lions, one crouching at each corner of the tower, guarding its base; their muzzles are drawn back in a snarl, fangs exposed, and tongues loll out terrifyingly. All around the outside of the tower were friezes depicting mythological scenes; only fragments survive, but enough to show that a complicated mythology was being depicted. The interpretation of the oriental iconography is exceedingly difficult since there are no specific written texts to help, and the finest panels are only parts of larger compositions. It is by no means certain that all belong to this tomb.

Martín Almagro describes the scenes in this way. The first is set in hell (*ill. 68*). A monstrous divinity presides, seated on a lion-footed throne. He has a corpulent human body with two heads ending in large snouts with protruding tongues; in his right hand he holds a deep bowl from which a little person peeps out, with just his head and feet showing; his left hand grasps a dead boar laid out on a table before him. Behind the boar stands a figure facing the throne, sticking out its forked tongue; it too holds a deep bowl identical to the one held by the enthroned deity. The long fringed tunic and pointed cap hint that it is a female. On the extreme right-hand side is another figure with a tight belt giving it a pinched waist, and having an equine head; it holds a large curved knife in one hand, and another bowl with a little person in it, resting on a table. This is a truly awful scene, set in the underworld, where offerings are made to the monstrous divinities, the Lords of the Dead. It is not a banquet, or a procession, but a frightening vision of the Lord of the Dead as the devourer of men. Perhaps the little person in the bowl is the tomb's occupant. The mythology and symbolism is clearly oriental, with important detail such as the boar as a funerary offering documented from Phoenician rites in the east Mediterranean.

The second panel depicts a heavily muscled figure dressed in a short tunic, striding forward (*ill. 69*). Facing him is a fierce animal belching fire, or bellowing with all its might. Behind the figure is a fallen tree in which perch eight plump little birds, and below it are three small men with pointed noses, two of whom have sharp forks which they thrust upwards into the tree; the third man follows the main figure. On the far right are more monsters spitting fire, but their bodies must have been depicted on the adjoining panel which has not been found. Part of a thick serpent's body is just visible below them. The scene is quite different in content and tone from the first one. The main figure is that of a hero, or super-human; the tree may be the Tree of Life so common in oriental mythology, defended by fierce monsters. Their terrific natures contrast with the apparent tranquility of the scene. Almagro's interpretation was that the hero had robbed the Tree of Life and was fleeing its guardian beasts, who were attacking him.

Several smaller enigmatic frieze fragments were found, including an armoured warrior who may be identified as the 'Smiting God' or Reshef; a scene with an explicit sexual coupling; a marine monster or giant serpent; and a figure seated near a large lotus flower. But the best-preserved of all is a relief from the uppermost part of the tower, depicting a boar with a head before and behind, fighting twin creatures depicted as serpent-bodied humans (*ill. 70*). The complete, symmetrical nature of this scene shows it was designed as a centre-piece, and it has been interpreted as a heraldic relief rather than a mythical scene.

This detailed description is necessary to come to terms with the extraordinary nature of this monument. Pozo Moro is clear evidence of a rationalized, orderly architecture in the far west, and can really only be explained by the existence of great buildings still older, such as the Herakleion (the temple of Melkart) near Cadiz. Without such models it is hard to explain the appearance of such a clever and complete monument as Pozo Moro, much less its elaborate mythical scenes. The oriental mythology, Phoenician in many concrete details, is clear and was likely transmitted through colonists in southern Spain and Cadiz, even though it is not completely faithful in its detail. The temple of Melkart (discussed in Chapter 9) not only had the architectural elements on display but also the ten labours of Melkart sculpted on its main doors. Prototypes of Phoenician myths and legends in sculpted form were therefore on hand, with oriental myths recreated in the far west by the Phoenicians, and later imitated by Iberian people who would change some of their details.

The mythical narratives on the Pozo Moro friezes were probably intended to confirm the heroic, or even divine, personality of the dead man buried in the tomb, and, consequently, the sacred nature of his own power and wealth. This is exactly the sort of legitimization of power that Max Weber identified when he discussed the origins of ruling elites and the manner in which they consolidated their authority once they had gained it. The owner of the Pozo Moro tomb sought to do this by stressing that his power stemmed ultimately from a divine source, and had a sacred authority conferred upon it; these claims would be taken up

**67–70 The tomb of Pozo Moro** (*Above*) The reconstruction of the tomb as it is today in the Museo Arqueológico Nacional in Madrid. Although it incorporates most of the sculptures into a single monument, many scholars believe that they come from different constructions. The base and the lions seem pretty certain; the rest is more conjectural. (*Right, top*) Carved panel, perhaps depicting hell, with a monstrous divinity seated on his throne, presiding over the Lords of the Dead. (*Right, centre*) Another carved panel showing a figure striding towards the left with a fallen tree behind him. (*Right, bottom*) Stone panel depicting a boar with a head fore and behind, fighting twin creatures. It may be a heraldic device.

by his heirs and successors as they attempted to maintain their own position and the power that accompanied them. It may be extravagant to term these pretensions sacred kingships like the oriental ones, but such institutions were known in several Phoenician city-states; since they are general and widespread features, the concept of a sacred kingship fits well with the tomb's iconography. Above all else, these ideas give the building and decoration of the tomb a specific purpose which would be missing otherwise; these dread and frightening scenes were not intended as just aesthetic touches.

## Friezes from Porcuna

Another splendid tomb has been located at Porcuna (ancient Obulco) in the province of Jaén – or perhaps more accurately, scores of fine sculptures in limestone belonging to a great tomb have been discovered built into modern field walls at the site. At least forty figures are represented, and although they lack the detailed archaeological context that makes the Pozo Moro so valuable, they represent a level of sculptural achievement and technical ability unsurpassed in Iberia. The Porcuna sculptures mark a notable advance on the Pozo Moro lions and reliefs both technically and ideologically. The sculptures are about half life-size, mostly freestanding, and many carved in groups resting on the same base. They are entirely different in style from the native Iberian sculpture found in the same area, and judging by their perfection could be the work of a Greek craftsman working between 450 and 400 BC. The themes are less complicated to describe and identify than the Pozo Moro ones, partly on account of their greater realism and sculptural accuracy, and partly because there are no large combinations or scenes that can be reconstructed.

The best pieces from Porcuna include a detailed carving of an armoured warrior (*ills. 72–75*); another holding his horse by the reins as it pulls hard; one struggling with a fierce griffin; and a fourth of a hunter carrying a hare. Detached pieces include a fine helmeted head (*ill. 71*), a large statue of Artemis with a deer on each side of her, at least two fine recumbent bulls and a well-detailed horse's head. The construction of this tomb – or perhaps it should be described as a '*Heroön*' (i.e. shrine to a hero) if it really was devoted to an heroized man – represents an iconographic development of the prevailing mythology. It is not only later than Pozo Moro, and distinct in tone and content, but stresses human, rather than divine images. This suggests a change in ideology too, perhaps coinciding with a phase of strong Greek influence in southern Spain, climaxing in the period 400 to 350 BC. The mythical scenes of the warrior hero, sometimes mounted on horseback, the hunts, fights and feasts realistically depicted, all show this. The latest examples of these huge tombs such as the ones at Alcoy, Pinohermoso, or Osuna A,

71 Head of helmeted man carved in stone from Porcuna.

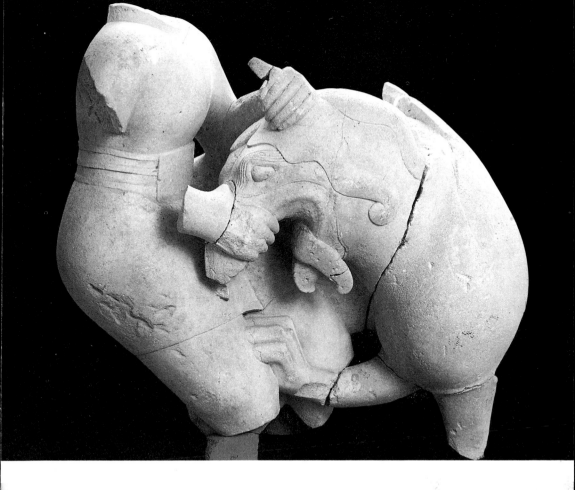

72–75 **Sculpture from Porcuna** (*Left*, *above*) a hunter dressed in a tunic and carrying a hare in his right hand, with a large dog behind him; (*left*, *below*) sculpture showing an armoured warrior pulling hard at the reins of his horse. (*Above*) A man engaged in a fierce struggle with a griffin which claws at his thigh; (*right*) an armoured warrior who carries his circular shield slung before him.

76 (*Left*) A reconstruction of an Iberian funerary sculpture of a bull on a pedestal or column, from Monforte de Cid (Alicante). Height as restored is about 3 m. Date in fourth century BC.

77 (*Right*) This stone carving of a crouching lion from Nueva Carteya (León, Cordoba) is one of the most expressive beasts that have survived. It was probably once part of the base of a tower tomb like Pozo Moro, and dates to the fifth century BC.

show a preference for increasing realism in the depiction of funerary ritual. The preferred themes involve familiar participants: riders, warriors, bulls, lions or deer, engaged in games, fights or dances. There are still mythological scenes, of course, as at Porcuna, and these last down to the third century. Accompanying this greater realism in sculpture is an increase in the range and richness of geometric plant motifs in the architectural schemes. This is paralleled by a growing popularity for these designs in other fields of artistic expression, such as painted pottery and decorated metalwork (especially large belt buckles).

## A break in tradition

Iberian architecture stops suddenly in the third century in southeast Spain where it had formerly flourished. It continued in Andalusia, and notable monuments continued to be built into the period of Roman dominion. The truncation of such a vigorous art style and monumental form may be related to the wave of destruction that some archaeologists see in the villages of the area at the end of the fourth century, and which others ascribe to changes in colonial commerce which left the former elites deprived of their sources of wealth.

The other class of important architectural monument is the decorated stela, or freestanding pillar. Almagro was the first to recognize that this, too, is a widespread architectural form which was consistently decorated with sculpture and adorned with geometrically carved capitals and shafts.

He has identified over 200 such pillars in an area stretching from Sagunto to Seville, and ranging in time from the sixth to the first centuries. They were simple monuments, averaging 3 m tall, often with a single piece of freestanding sculpture on the top (*ill. 76*). They usually occur singly in Iberian cemeteries, but a few have been found grouped together; the largest group so far located is at Cabezo Lucero (Alicante) where no less than six were discovered, possibly set up in an alignment. The oldest example seems to be that of a sphinx from a pillar monument from the Punic settlement at Villaricos, dated to the sixth century. This points out again that the origin of the monumental pillar is oriental, in this case, specifically Phoenician, rather than Greek.

Sculptured tombs were often placed in isolated localities, far from major settlements. This emphasizes the lack of sculpture in Iberian domestic contexts, and no public building, fortification, or temple built by the Iberians has been found decorated in this manner. Pozo Moro, Pinohermoso, and Alcoy, rich tower tombs all three, stand in isolated localities. They seem to have been set up sporadically, as the need arose, because there is no evidence that permanent schools of craftsmen were maintained. Taking into account that Iberian sculpture lasted for nearly 600 years and covers a huge territory, it is not surprising that its style and quality of carving vary. But even more obviously, sculpture was used as decoration for a specific architectural context with a graphic symbolism. Many of the isolated lions and unidentifiable beasts must come from funerary monuments and pillars now destroyed (*ill. 77*).

# 9 · The new gods

So MUCH OF the sculpture and jewellery that has survived was originally intended for religious purposes, that it is impossible to interpret, or even describe properly, without knowing at least a little about the new gods – new, that is, to the Iberians. The cults and deities we recognize are all foreign ones, mostly Phoenician, since we have textual sources referring to them in the eastern Mediterranean. Our ignorance about practices and beliefs in the later Bronze Age among the indigenous peoples is simply that: a lack of factual evidence which does not imply there were no established cults already in place.

The Phoenician pantheon was elaborate and functional, and astral cults played no part in it. Among the chief deities, who appeared under many guises, was a protective god of the city, who might be named as El, Baal, or Melkart, and a goddess who was his consort, recognizable as Astarte or Tanit, responsible for the fertile earth. To the Greeks she was similar to Persephone. A developed iconography specifies their attributes, so we can follow them in the archaeological record. The cults were practised near water, large trees, groves, mountain tops and other places considered sacred, and sacrifices made with animal and vegetal offerings; these included human sacrifices, although it must be said that no Phoenician human sacrifices have been found in Spain.

Iberians began to adopt the new pantheon with real enthusiasm early on; or at least we can say that they adopted the accoutrements and outward paraphernalia with gusto, since the orientalizing period is one expression of this, insofar as it is part of the desire to ape Phoenician values for personal advantage. In the Balearics this model was a Punic one; in Catalonia Greek, with different effects in each case. So Iberian religion has come down to us as a cultural phenomenon, expressed in diverse ways that are often bizarre, or at the least, capable of more than one explanation. First we see a ragbag of objects and ideas being copied, then a more standardized interest in rituals, and finally as something we can look at iconographically as representing Iberian religious experience without knowing what it was, or its values were. It can be seen in operation as folk worship at open-air shrines, or through the affection for potent Egyptian charms with their alien magic, or in cults of the dead. Much though we describe and conjecture, the system of beliefs is well nigh impossible to restore. Our greatest success has been in understanding the uses to which the new iconography was put.

78 The Phoenician temple of Melkart near Cadiz probably looked like this reconstruction of Solomon's temple in Jerusalem. The similarity between them has long been commented upon. Solomon's temple was designed and furnished by Phoenician craftsmen, sent to him by his brother-in-law, Hiram, king of Tyre. The decorated doors would have been the chief sculptural ornament, flanked by two freestanding bronze columns bearing cressets; they would be about 12 m tall. The building would have been lit by windows placed just below the eaves, which was an Egyptian architectural technique.

## The Temple of Melkart near Cadiz (the Herakleion)

The first great temple built in Spain was the work of the Phoenicians, specifically those from Tyre; we can say this with some certainty, since the religious beliefs and observances of late Bronze Age societies took place in settings of material simplicity. No cult buildings have been found, and if beliefs did require consecrated settings for public rites and ceremonies, they are still undiscovered. The images seen on the rock paintings common to much of southern and eastern Spain hardly seem sufficient to support an elaborate mythological world, and Bronze Age Spain is noted for its aniconic features. Against this background of iconographic simplicity, the sudden interest in buildings for public worship and cult places that is detectable after the eighth century is all the more interesting, for it shows unambiguously the practical effects that contact with Phoenician and Greek societies produced.

The most detailed documentation that survives for any early religious building in the far west concerns the temple built outside Gadir, dedicated to the god Melkart, and known to later Greek writers as the Herakleion. This was the principal temple to the great Phoenician deity in the west, and was famous throughout the ancient world from at least 500 BC. The site of this building and its shrines is today lost to sight, covered by the waters and sands of the islet of Sancti Petri, and a description has to rely entirely on historical sources from later Graeco-Roman writers, and comparison with the temple of Solomon in Jerusalem, described in detail in the biblical account in the first chapter of the Book of Kings (*ill. 78*). Its archaeological and cultural importance is that it served as a model and source of artistic inspiration to the Iberian people in southern Spain.

The cult of Melkart was especially strong in Tyre; the name Melkart means 'king of the city' in the Phoenician language. He was depicted as a god who created life in the spring then perished under the scorching heat of the summer sun as does the Mediterranean vegetation. Later he acquired attributes as protector of mariners and merchants, and by 600 BC was identified by the Greeks with their own hero, Herakles. The feats of Melkart and the labours of Herakles became entwined as one mythical cycle.

The Herkaleion was located 18 km from Gadir, at the far end of a long, thin island which had the city at the northern end and the shrine at the other, connected by a road. The site today is known as Sancti Petri, a rocky islet isolated from the main island by two millennia of coastal erosion on the seaward side. It is formed of a conglomerate rock, rising about 3 m above high-tide level, and still measures 400 by 500 m, although it was formerly larger. Despite its inhospitable appearance, Sancti Petri has permanent fresh-water springs; Gadir also had fresh water from shallow wells. These were replenished constantly because the rock formation stretches across to the mainland, and taps large acquifers there. These springs must have been a principal attraction of the island to the earliest Phoenician mariners.

The Classical descriptions of this site agree that there was a large temple, built in the Phoenician style of architecture; that it was very old, with huge timber beams in the roof; and that the rites and sacrificial rituals associated with it were purely Phoenician. We may conjecture that there was a large open patio, possibly colonnaded in oriental fashion, with the temple building at one end, a freestanding altar before it, with lesser altars, temples, and memorials within it. Ancient writers said that the temple covered the entire island, but since this is clearly impossible, it is likely they were referring to the sacred enclosure, or *temenos*.

The chief details of the temple that attracted interest were the decorated doors, bearing the scenes of Herakles and Melkart. These were listed by the Roman writer Silius Italicus in the first century BC as depicting the following myths: the Hydra of Lerna; the Nemean Lion; Cerberus the Hound of Hell; the Man-eating Horse of Diomedes, King of Thrace; the Erymanthean Boar, and the Copper-hoofed Doe of Kyrenea. They are all part of the cycle of legendary labours common to Herakles and Melkart. The last four labours were not part of the Greek cycle, and included panels depicting the prostrate giant, Antaeus; a centaur, Nessos; and Acheleous, the Human-headed Ox. The last panel showed the apotheosis of the hero (Melkart) on Mt Oeta. The fact that there are only ten scenes, and not the twelve that were later canonized in all depictions of the Heraklian myths after the third century, suggests that these doors were made at a time before the legends had settled into a fixed cycle of twelve, and also that there was a common oriental origin for the myths of both heroes. There is another point to make about these depictions, though: they signally lack the labours of Herakles that were traditionally (before 600 BC) set in the far west by the Greeks, such as the theft of the Hesperian apples leaving Atlas bearing the heavens on his shoulders, or Herakles's fight with Geryon the three-headed man! So, if the sculptors had had the Greek labours of Hercules in mind while they wrought the doors, it would have been extremely odd if they had neglected those legends most directly connected with their western homelands. For this reason we suspect that the subject matter concerned the god Melkart, not Herakles.

If we assume that Silius Italicus's description is correct, as it may be, given the precise detail, then we must seek an interpretation for it. One modern attempt of great ingenuity by the Russian scholar J. B. Tsirkin treats the scenes as a single iconographical cycle of essentially nine acts, in three groups of three, where the hero battles with frightful monsters of the ocean, upon land, and deep down beneath it; they represent the powers of death, conquered in turn by the indomitable Melkart. He dies to destroy his infirm old age in flames, and is resurrected, renewed as a youth, rising from the fire. The ten panels of the Herakleion would then represent the nine fights paving the way for the climax, that of the hero's apotheosis; the light of the universe triumphs over the darkness of death in all its terrible forms.

Carvings like these, in a monumental setting and open to public view, would have been in the Phoenician style, quite properly for Phoenician myths depicting one of their greatest deities, and would have been a powerfully attractive prototype for sculptors desirous of making their own works.

The other outstanding physical features of this building were the pillars of Herakles, a term which even in ancient times was used without clear distinction to refer to the rocks of Gebel Musa and Gibraltar framing the Straits of Gibraltar; or perhaps a pair of small, plain stone columns used as altars inside the temple; or even the imposing pillared façade of the sanctuary. It is the pillars on this façade which are of immediate interest. One stood on each side of the main door, both inscribed with an unintelligible script that could not be read even by the priests serving in the temple. These pillars can be paralleled in Solomon's temple built between 961 and 922 BC, where columns flanked the main door, and were crowned with huge cressets from which fires might blaze or perfumes be consumed. These stood about 10.5 m tall, and were called Boaz and Jachin, derived perhaps from the first words on the inscriptions they bore. The ones in the Herakleion were probably similar.

Writers also agree that the temple contained no cult image at all. Within the patio around the temple building were two springs of sweet water, used for ablutions, an olive tree which fanciful writers imagined fruited with emeralds instead of edible olives, an oracle, and probably a repository for the temple treasure. The rituals were still markedly Phoenician even in Julius Caesar's time, and the priests served barefooted, shaven-headed, clothed in white linen robes decorated with purple fringes. There is no convincing evidence of human sacrifices, and certainly nothing like the *tophets* of Carthage or Sardinia where children were systematically sacrificed.

It is impossible to establish the date of the Herakleion's foundation exactly; one clue may be found in the three bronze statuettes recently dredged up off the seabed in shallows near the sanctuary. One of them is like the archaic statuette of Reshef found off shore at Sciacca in Sicily and dated to the eleventh century. The other two are better preserved, and very Egyptian in style; there is a bearded man with a tiara and short skirt, and a youth, clean shaven, with a crown. All had lugs on their feet for attachment to a pedestal, and their date could lie in the eighth to the seventh centuries, like the pair found at the Punta Umbría in the Ría de Huelva (*see ill. 25*). A date of 700 BC is therefore a conservative one for the founding of some sanctuary at Sancti Petri, since the statuettes are likely to have belonged to it. A related problem is the date of the foundation of Gadir, which has been an unresolved controversy for centuries. At the moment, there are no Phoenician finds older than 600 BC from the city, but we should not be too shocked if finds far older come to light to confirm the traditional foundation date of 1100 BC. Gadir was also the seat of at least two more temples, the chief being the Kronion: about this sanctuary we remain in complete ignorance.

## Iberian shrines

Our view of popular religion is unusually vivid thanks to half a dozen rich sanctuaries in eastern Andalusia full of *ex votos* of bronze, stone and clay. They give a very different picture of Iberian religious beliefs than the elaborate funerary sculptures and the modest little temple at Illeta dels Banyets (Alicante). Three of these sanctuaries yielded nearly 6000 bronze figurines, and another trio provided 800 stone and clay sculptures.

The sanctuary at the Collado de los Jardines is the best-known and most enigmatic of all of them. Located in the defile of Despeñaperros, it overlooks the main route through the Sierra Morena linking the Guadalquivir valley with the inland Mesetas (*ill. 79*). The site covers a large area, and has many separate components which we cannot relate to each other with much precision. There are two rock shelters with painted scenes dating to the Bronze Age within shouting distance of a third, which forms the Iberian sanctuary proper. The large rock shelter may once have been a cave with a pool in its recesses, communicating with the spring that still flows down the lower slope. From a deep rubbish dump just outside this shelter, Juan Cabré dug up 2200 bronze figurines in his excavations between 1916 and 1919, and another 1300 were recovered by other diggers. A stone terrace may have supported a small temple immediately outside the shelter, and there was certainly a later building, probably Roman, with some architectural pretensions, including column bases and capitals. Above the rock shelter, forming a small settlement around an acropolis, were clusters of rectangular houses, nearly all with signs that bronze casting had taken place inside them, and a cremation cemetery. Figurines were found in the cemetery, but not actually in tombs. The whole area was enclosed by a stone wall that guarded more than 30 ha; that is, a space measuring about 800 by 380 m.

The offerings that have always caught most attention are the human and animal figurines, all cast in bronze by the lost wax method, and most around 10 to 12 cm tall (*ill. 80*). Their subject matter is extremely varied, but over 95 per cent are human figures; Cabré's calculations give 3 per cent armed warriors, 54 per cent men, and 39 per cent women. They included tonsured priests, people making offerings, naked men, and people praying. Other important categories include at least 400 bronze brooches, many Roman coins, including issues of the fifth century AD, and a lot of simple *ex votos* of breasts, limbs, feet, eyes, and teeth. Pottery and animal bones were found in the rubbish dump. The date of these finds has been controversial since they were first observed in the eighteenth century. Modern studies by Gérard Nicolini show that some statuettes are close to Phoenician models around 600 BC; more schematic ones would be much later, perhaps of Roman date. The sanctuary was used for about a thousand years, and perhaps twice as long as that if one includes the painted rock shelters nearby. What were all these figures doing in the sanctuary? The usual explanation is that they were truly *ex votos*, that is, gifts made to a deity as thank offerings for favours granted in return for requests made in prayers. The choice of a human figure, dressed or not, would therefore represent the worshipper offering himself to the deity in a spirit of gratitude, a token of his affection for the divinity. The excavators believed, too, that the walled area was a sacred wood connected with the shrine, and that figurines were dangled from branches of trees within it; this seems improbable.

A similar site lies at Castellar de Santisteban, 35 km away in the same province of Jaén, where rock shelters and springs occur. One rock shelter was the sanctuary, and in a rubbish dump just below it were found over 2000 bronze figurines. They seem locally made. The third sanctuary with bronze figurines is at Nuestra Señora de Luz, 6 km south of the city of Murcia, where a low hillock was topped by a shrine built on a terrace. Hundreds of statuettes came from rubbish contexts close by (*ill. 81*). It too had a spring. Another thirty locations in Spain have similar figurines, but only as individual pieces; the remarkable concentration centres upon just three sanctuaries.

**79–81 Shrine and bronze statuettes**
(*Above*) A view of the shrine and acropolis of Collado de los Jardines. The cave is in the centre left of the picture. (*Right*) A Phoenician statue cast in bronze from Medina de las Torres (Badajoz). From its pose, dress, and long sidelocks of neatly dressed hair, it is thought to represent the god Reshef, lord of lightning, the smiter. Bronze figures of this quality could have been made in Cadiz, or imported from Phoenicia between 700 and 600 BC. They provided models and stimuli for the Iberians to copy in their own figurines at Collado de los Jardines (Jaén), whose series starts around 600 BC. (*Far right*) An Iberian bronze statuette of a man dressed in a belted tunic, cap, and bearing a lance (how lost). Statues like this were found in their thousands at the sanctuary of Collado de los Jardines. This example comes from Nuestra Señora de Luz (Murcia).

128

The origin of these shrines poses a problem that Nicolini tries hard to solve. He suggested that the Collado de los Jardines sanctuary began with priests establishing a foreign cult there; as time passed their influence faded and finally withered entirely, as local people made offerings of their own choice and style. This idea accounted for the twenty early statuettes of tonsured priests who seem to be akin to the Phoenician ones known both from bronze statuettes like one from Cadiz with a golden face, and from later written accounts of those who served at the Herakleion. Only three priests' statuettes come from Castellar, and none from Nuestra Señora de Luz, which is the most recent of the three sites. Of course, the question which we most wish to be answered is the one hardest to resolve:

why should foreign cults be set up at Collado de los Jardines in the first place, and if successfully, why did they die out?

The other sanctuaries are of a different stamp. At the Cerro de los Santos close to Montealegre (Murcia) over 300 stone sculptures were taken from a ruined and looted temple. This building lasted into the later Roman period and the sculptures are undatable except by their style. However, there are ten small statues of seated ladies on thrones or high chairs, another sixteen ladies making offerings, and many fragments of men's heads (*ill. 84*). Some, at least, belong to the fourth to the third centuries. Other *ex votos* of bulls, cows and horses in stone and bronze were dug up in the 1870s, along with a pair of bronze statuettes like the ones from Collado de los Jardines; a dump of about 200 iron lanceheads in a rocky hollow was also located. A similar sanctuary on a low hill at El Cigarralejo near Mula, also in Murcia, yielded 175 small stone sculptures of horses, fifteen other equids, and seventeen humans, all dated to the fourth to the second centuries. They too were found in a dump, and broken into pieces (*ills. 82, 83*). So many horsey *ex votos* inclined the excavator to interpret them as offerings to a deity who was worshipped as the protector of horses, guarantor of their fertility, health and abundance. Indeed, the horse is almost the sole object of veneration at this sanctuary. Clay sculptures come from the Serreta de Alcoy located on a hill near Alicante; they also come from a trash heap, are undatable, and comprise at least 300 human figurines.

What all these sites have in common is a distinctive quality where the worshipper acted directly before his deity, without the mediation of a professional priesthood, making his offering directly and in person; the human figures are the worshippers presenting themselves to their deity. The sanctuaries do not have sumptuously embellished temples, or divine images even in miniature form, and most strikingly of all, there are no altars or sacrificial places. These sacred localities were chosen apparently by no fixed rule that we can discern; the mass-produced, repetitive bronze figures especially, indicate the popular style of the cult. While we can see the assimilation of Phoenician or Greek ideas in the manner of making *ex votos*, and their use, it is in fact a newly created need where none had existed before; nor is any oriental god set up in any of these places. They are indigenous, Iberian retreats where humble people could beseech their protectors directly for comfort and help. This is the context in which the thousands of bronze figurines need to be interpreted in the future. Each sanctuary had a specialized subject matter and medium; stone work is not found at Collado de los Jardines, nor bronzes at Cigarralejo.

In the Spanish Levant the place of sanctuaries is taken by caves in high and remote places, inaccessible to all but the most determined visitor. They are believed to be sites where cult offerings were made, but direct evidence is still thin.

82 (*Above*) Small stone sculpture of a bridled horse from the sanctuary of Cigarralejo (Mula, Murcia).

83 (*Above, top*) Group of small stone sculptures of horses from the sanctuary of Cigarralejo (Mula, Murcia).

84 (*Above, right*) A stone sculpture of a lady – perhaps a priestess – making an offering. It comes from the sanctuary of Cerro de los Santos (Albacete).

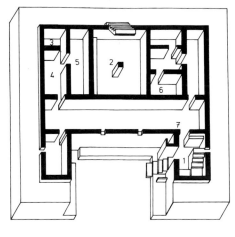

85 A plan of the monument at Cancho Roano (Badajoz). The entire structure measures 24 m on each side. The building is of mud bricks, surrounded by a wide terrace revetted in stone, which stands 2.5 m high. It was modified to hold the ash fillings, and the entrance, as well as the door opening on to the terrace (*1*), had been blocked with mud bricks. The mass of ashes filled every room except the 'blind' one with a central brick pillar, which had sterile earth dumped in it (*2*). Important discoveries dating to the use of the building included caches of amphoras of local manufacture; six were found filled with beans and wheat (*3*), and next door another sixteen held wine, and rested on a slate floor (*4*). In the ash filling were burned pieces of carved furniture inlaid with bone, and decorated with bronze figurines and claw feet (*5*). A clay pot with a silver bowl and gold earrings in it lay just behind the staircase ascending to the terrace. Personal possessions of a humbler kind were a set of bone gaming pieces (*6*), and some iron weapons from the only warrior burial (*7*). All of these items are dated to between 450 and 375 BC.

## Cancho Roano (Badajoz)

The most recently discovered sanctuary is the building excavated since 1978 at Cancho Roano (Badajoz). The site is a low promontory overlooking the permanent watercourse of the Cigancha river, and at one end, apparently all by itself and free from other buildings or settlement, lies the sanctuary (*ill. 85*). It is a massive structure, designed and built at one time, forming a rough square about 24 m long on each side, and composed of two monumental elements; a mud-brick building at the core, standing to a height of nearly 4 m, and an enclosing terrace of cyclopean construction 2.5 m high and wide. From afar the site appears like the bottom of a stepped pyramid.

There is a courtyard from which a stairway enters a vestibule to reach the main floor level, 1.4 m higher than the ground. The mud-brick walls were faced with irregular slabs of blue slate inside and out, and the floors of the main hall and courtyard were also slabbed over with this stone; other rooms were simply lined with a thin clay plaster or pale cream wash. On the northern side of the main vestibule a staircase allowed easy access to the main terrace, which runs right round the building. No internal features were found, nor traces of roofing elements.

Traces of an earlier stone and clay building, called an 'oratory' or 'crypt' by the excavator, lie deep below the main floor, and have not been explored further. It may be an earlier monument.

But the outstanding feature of the building is its filling. Every room except one was filled from the floor to the tops of the walls with ash; ash from scores of fierce wood fires which had burned on the narrow pavement outside the cyclopean terrace, and which was interspersed with thin bands of clay. The original entrances from the courtyard were blocked up with mud bricks in order that the ashes might be better contained within the building. The volume of this ash is tremendous, and amounts to at least 540 cubic metres!

Artefacts that belong to the period when the sanctuary was built and used, rather than from its ashy contents, are few and modest; they include a few quernstones and about two-dozen amphoras found leaning against the walls of two rooms by the farmer who had discovered the site. At the base of the stairway in the courtyard was a large iron tethering ring.

Much more impressive were the discoveries made in the ash, where thousands of pottery fragments were scattered in utter disorder throughout the building. There are some remarkable things here: at least nine Greek red-figure wine cups, made in Attica, and pieces of another 150 or so of simpler design, also imported from Greece. There were many amphoras too, and an unusual range of personal possessions, from gaming pieces to sealstones, to fine bronzes that belong to horse tackle, and even a pair of legs from a large bronze statue of a goat. But what are we to make of the carbonized remains of decorated furniture, or the humble objects like loom weights and more than 1000 spindlewhorls and knucklebones? Surely all of these cannot be funerary offerings. However, the bulk of the finer objects are evidently not the sort of things left behind by everyday chores in the home.

Now this tremendous building and its astonishing fill of ash pose problems that archaeologists alone may be incapable of interpreting correctly. The excavator, Juan Maluquer de Motes of Barcelona University, believed he had found a great sanctuary, or even a palace, which fell into disuse and was later appropriated as a repository for the ashes left-over from the funeral pyres on which dead Lusitanians (i.e. Portuguese) were cremated; their bones were then separated and buried in a small cemetery close by. In other words, he thought the site had at least two periods of use with entirely different functions. But even before he had published more than a provisional note on Cancho Roano, an alternative interpretation was offered by Antonio Blanco Freijeiro, who saw the monument as a gigantic ash altar; that is, a kind of structure known from Classical writers to have existed at Olympia from the eighth century, formed by accreting the ashes from offerings burned on altars of sacrifice, and cementing them together with a small amount of clay, blood or calcium-rich water. Only two small ash altars have been dug in the ancient world, and neither is like Cancho Roano. Nor are there many monumental altars the size of Cancho Roano, and those that we know have quite different interior arrangements. Blanco supports his case with references from Strabo, writing about Lusitanian customs of sacrifice, and the description of the Greek traveller Pausanius who saw the long-vanished altar of Zeus at Olympia. This is an unconvincing argument. It ignores the two clear phases of construction and use of the site, and it presumes a level of ritual sophistication that requires the wholesale adoption of alien rites from the Greek world. We know that Lusitanian society was pastoral and without any urban centres such as those long-established in the Guadalquivir valley. The cult of ash altars, of hallowing spots with sacred ash heaps, was a Greek one, and part of the general Greek practice of making sacrifices as the focal point of public rituals. It is hard to believe that such rites would fit in easily to a society organized at the level of chieftains and clans, and even less that Cancho Roano is an example of this.

What is Cancho Roano? Is it a sanctuary, or even a temple? It has more than one building phase, since stone walls have been found below its floor level. The plan looks just like that of a large, well-ordered house, which had been sited prominently and decorated inside and out with stone slabs. It has no close parallels in the western Mediterranean, and is one of the larger individual buildings found outside the Classical world. For these reasons, Maluquer de Motes looked for parallels in Syria, and thought of a palace. If it is the house of a prosperous family then it is likely to have belonged to a settlement, the remains of which have been eroded, or simply not discovered.

The ash fills of the last period of its use have been radiocarbon dated to around 400 BC, and judging by their complicated stratigraphy, were formed by repeated tippings of ash scooped from a funeral pyre upon which offerings had been made. The presence of a few graves of the same date just on the edge of the monument suggests that a large, and perhaps rich, cemetery might be found. The artefacts are datable to the period 430–375 BC by the Greek pottery, although there is a scatter of older material from outside the excavation. The crude digging technique denies us valuable detail on the ash fill; we do not know how many events are represented, nor their periodicity, nor even the contents of a single act of sacrifice made at one moment, yet the opportunity was there to find these things out. Without these essential observations our chances of understanding the rituals and acts connected with them are remote; we have to treat the acts together as one; all that is certain about the rituals is the concrete detail that was large and clear. Thus we learn about the amphoras full of wheat, beans, and wine in the storage rooms (the latter stank when it was brought into contact with the fresh air), the common occurrence of almonds and pine nuts, and some animal bones, chiefly from goats. There are notably few weapons or human remains; the dominating aspect of the rituals is that of rich banquets accompanied by wine, cake or bread. We have no inkling of the nature of the divinity to whom these were made.

As a unique monument Cancho Roano defies our present understanding, but we must not be surprised if it turns out to be the house of a wealthy family, probably in a settlement, later reused as the focus of an accompanying cemetery.

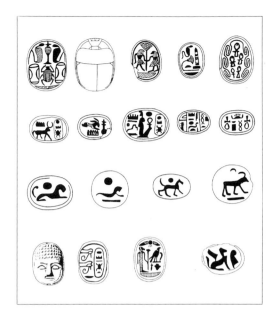

86 A selection of sixteen Egyptian scarabs found in Iberia. The first and second rows come from graves on Ibiza, chiefly the cemetery of Puig des Molins; row 3 illustrates four scarabs from the Iberian cemetery of Can Canyis (Tarragona), and row 4 has three scarabs from Portugal. That on the left is from Porto do Sabugeiro, while the two on the right are from graves in the cemetery at Alcácer do Sal. Their dates are between 550 and 400 BC.

## Egyptian magic

Magical charms from Egypt form a class of article different from all the others brought in by Phoenicians and Carthaginians. The glass paste amulets come mostly from Ibizan graves, and are one of the Carthaginian customs which the island followed so closely. The other charms are scarabs or sealstones made and engraved in Egypt, found in graves from Catalonia to Cadiz and across to central Portugal (*ill. 86*). Some were already 800 or 900 years old when they were exported westwards. Ibiza has the most, although there are important groups in the Iberian cemetery at Can Canyis (Tarragona), Villaricos, Gorham's Cave (Gibraltar) (which may have been a Phoenician shrine), and Cadiz. Specialists who have examined these seals minutely are convinced that they were chosen for their magical properties, their 'power', and not for any novelty value as baubles. Their reasons for this are that the scarabs are exclusively funerary goods, used chiefly by women and children, just as among the lower classes in Egypt, for whom they represented safeguards into the next world. The subjects on the seals vary greatly at the start of their importation, then narrow down to a few themes, as if the users had found some deities whom they regarded as especially potent. The scarabs were used from 550 to 400 BC, when they ceased to be imported; the same thing happened in Carthage, where a third of all graves in the seventh to the sixth centuries contained a scarab, yet they decreased in popularity until they vanished entirely as grave goods around 400 BC.

This superstitious interest in the occult power of Egyptian objects may explain the choice of a bronze statuette of Imhotep discovered in a *taula* (i.e. an apsidal stone building with a central pillar, unique to the island of Menorca in the Balearics) at the Torre d'En Gaumes (Menorca), where he had been put in a stone cist along with a few simple surgical implements (*ill. 87*). The context is sixth to the fifth centuries, and the statuette is part of the orientalizing phase on the Balearic Islands. Imhotep was the vizier of the Pharaoh Djoser, and was later deified as a god of medicine; this fact probably enhanced the statuette's virtues in the eyes of its Menorcan owners.

## Enthroned ladies

In July 1971 the celebrated statue now called the Dama de Baza was discovered in a grave in the Iberian cemetery of the Cerro del Santuario, near Baza (Jaén) (*ill. 88*). It was placed in a tomb that measured 2.6 m sq and 1.8 m deep, and had been carefully lowered into place against the north wall. In each corner of the vault was a Punic amphora connected to the surface by a funnel so that liquid offerings could be poured into it. Before the statue was a small pile of burned weapons and iron ornaments which had formed the panoply of a rich warrior, and elsewhere in the tomb were two plain bowls and a set of four elaborately painted vases with lids.

Two further tombs like this were identified in the same cemetery; one was looted but had a collapsed structure of wooden beams and adobe bricks in it; the other was intact and held rich grave goods including five Attic *kraters* with Dionysiac scenes, as well as four Punic amphoras, one in each corner to receive libations. The *kraters* were made between 400 and 375 BC, thereby giving a clue to the statue's date.

This splendid sculpture clears up several mysteries and engenders a new one. We can see now that the Dama de Elche, a far finer piece of stone carving, was once part of a similar funerary statue, since it is dressed in a like manner and has a cavity in the back to receive ashes or bones from a cremation (*see title page*). The group of seated ladies, or Damas, can be extended to include those from the Cabecico del Tesoro, Verdolay, and the Llano de la Consolación. Best of all, the discovery has laid to rest the vexed issue of the date of the Dama de Elche, and the whole school of fine sculpture related to her; it now belongs definitely in the fourth century, fittingly part of the climax of Iberian prosperity.

But whom do they represent? It is far from certain, and one can choose between seeing these ladies as representations of the goddess Persephone or Tanit, or as priestesses. The first choice is more logical in that we know that some of her attributes were to preserve life and fecundity in the underworld, making her the ideal champion to accompany a dead hero.

87 (*Above left*) A bronze statuette of Imhotep, the Egyptian god of medicine, from Torre d'En Gaumes, Menorca. The eyes are inlaid with gold, he wears a long pleated skirt, a rich broad collar, and sandals. A papyrus roll on his lap reads: 'Imhotep, son of Ptah, born of Hrdw-ñh'. The archaeological context is of the sixth to the fifth century BC, but the statuette is up to a century older.

88 The 'Dama de Baza', a statue of soft limestone weighing 800 kg and standing 1.3 m high, represents a seated lady, richly robed and bejewelled. Her throne is winged and lion-footed, and of a type well known in the Greek world. The entire statue was once coated with fine white plaster upon which the decoration of red, blue, brown and black was painted. She may be the Phoenician and Carthaginian goddess Astarte/Tanit, since she has that deity's symbol, a dove, in her hand. However, the closest overall parallels can be found in small seated models of the Greek goddess Persephone. The statue dates to between 400 and 350 BC. A cavity in the side was for the ashes of the dead man, indicating that one of its functions was that of a splendid funerary urn. Ill. 58 shows a side view of this statue.

137

89 This delicate alabaster carving of a seated lady flanked by sphinxes is Phoenician work of the seventh-century, and depicts the goddess Astarte/Tanit. Through a hole in the top of her head libations can be poured that spout from her breasts into the basin she holds before her. The statuette, or cult figure, was an heirloom at least 100 to 150 years old when it was finally consigned to the grave in the Iberian cemetery at Tutugi (Galera, Granada), accompanied by imported Greek pottery made between 550 and 500 BC.

The signs of Tanit were also used abundantly in Punic graves on Ibiza, not least on ostrich egg shells. We also possess suites of gold jewels from graves, like the one at Aliseda, admittedly of an earlier period, which are similar to those on the Damas of Baza and Elche; this could support an interpretation as priestesses (*ill. 89*).

## The Tivissa dish

Let us end this chapter with a few words about the greatest iconographic puzzle of all, the silver dish from Tivissa (*ills. 90–2*). If we knew certainly how to interpret the scenes, who the participants were, their qualities and particulars, then this single object could revolutionize the way we looked upon and thought about Iberian religion; for, in its way, this story is as important for Iberian mythology as the Gundestrup cauldron is for Celtic. The difference is that we have nothing similar to the archaic Old Irish legends to which to turn for guidance. Some interpret the scene as set in hell; others as a sacrifice and funerary feast; it may even be a simpler story altogether, with unconnected scenes, three separate acts, so to speak. There is no compelling reason why a single story should be depicted although iconographically it would be more interesting if it were. A simple interpretation might be that the three scenes show offerings (possibly first fruits) being made to an enthroned deity dressed in a cap and long robe followed by a hunt in which a mounted spearman attacks a lion feeding on a boar (the hunter in turn being hunted); lastly a lamb sacrifice, symbol of innocent purity. All the scenes are engraved in clear detail, down to distinctions between the hair of the centaurs, fur of wild cats, and the lion's mane.

90–92 **Tivissa iconography** Iberian cult scenes engraved on a large silver dish from Tivissa (Tarragona) and broadly dated to the third century BC. (*Top*) The first scene depicts an enthroned figure, offering what may be a small round fruit to a lesser person before him (or her). A squatting figure covering his ears is surrounded by three wild boars. Behind the throne is a centaur with a leafy branch and wild cat upon its back. (*Centre*) The second scene shows a mounted spearman juxtaposed with a lion eating a dead boar, while another wild cat plays with its tail. (*Bottom*) The third scene is peopled by winged men, one of whom is about to cut the throat of a lamb, while another stands before him with leafy branches sprouting from his hands. Behind him is a third winged man holding a stumpy tree, on which a bird, possibly an eagle, perches. In the centre of the plate (not shown) is a snarling wolf's head cast and chased in silver.

UNDECIPHERED LANGUAGES are one of the more intriguing archaeological riddles of the Iberians, and there are no less than two languages in three scripts that exist in written form. They continue to defy all attempts at decipherment. This does not mean they cannot be studied profitably, nor that valuable contextual information cannot be found in them, but it does give us a book whose pages remained sealed. The languages survive only as scripts carved on stone slabs, as graffiti on pottery and silver tableware, and a few flat lead sheets. Even the extraordinary qualities of the Basque language find only remote echoes in these Iberian ones; their antiquity, complexity and difficulty do not lessen their importance. Nor must we forget that our archaeological sample covers scripts written by peoples from the Algarve to Narbonne over a span of 800 years; more than enough time for important dialects and letter changes to emerge.

The oldest written languages in Iberia are not native ones but Egyptian and western Semitic; the first found on sealstones and alabaster jars brought from Egypt by Phoenician traders in the eighth century and later, and the second, which was the language used and written down by the Phoenicians themselves (*ill. 93*). These writing systems were known especially around the Río Tinto in the southwest and along the southern coast around Malaga. Another two centuries would pass before Greek scripts would be introduced into the far northeast of Spain by colonists at Emporion and Rhode after 575 BC. The Iberian scripts that developed under these oriental models form a writing system composed of twenty-eight, and towards the very end in the second century, twenty-nine, separate signs, making a semi-syllabic system that contained all the sound values required to represent accurately the indigenous spoken languages. These scripts were derived from Phoenician writing in the eighth century, and although modified their letter forms make an appreciably Semitic, rather than Greek, writing system.

Establishing the value of each sign was the work of Manuel Gómez Moreno, who in 1925 published his tables. The task was greatly eased by the discovery in 1908 at Ascoli (Italy) of a bronze tablet inscribed in Latin, containing the Iberian names of wealthy cavalrymen in the Ebro valley; in 1921 another stroke of luck yielded an Iberian text written in Greek letters of the Ionian alphabet from the shrine of La Serreta (Alcoy, Alicante); lastly, there were coins from the Roman Republican era with bilingual Iberian and Latin legends. These three sources allowed the values of the Iberian signs to be established satisfactorily. But from that

93 A bronze statuette of the goddess Astarte, with a dedicatory Phoenician inscription on the base. It comes from 'Seville', and was made around 700 BC.

time until today, all attempts at decipherment of the specific meaning of the texts has failed, thwarted by the non-Indo-European nature of the languages, the lack of long texts, and the absence of any lengthy bilingual inscriptions to help the code-breakers. From the phonetic values of the signs we can be fairly sure that the Iberian languages were not Indo-European, nor related to any branches of Celtic. There are no parallels with Etruscan, either. Where there are some phonetic values in common is, surprisingly, with the Basque language, now spoken only in the western Pyrenees and adjoining parts of the Cantabrian mountains. These similarities encouraged the idea that modern Basque was derived from ancient Iberian, reinforced by the knowledge that Basque too was non Indo-European and unique. So attempts were made to use modern Basque lexicons to translate 2300-year-old texts. This burlesque failed completely, and such parodies are best forgotten entirely. Iberian has to join Etruscan as one of the great linguistic puzzles of Europe.

## The mechanics of writing

The scripts fall into three main groups, all with the same semi-syllabic writing system; the southwest system is clearly the oldest, and is copied by that of the southeast, and by the latest, but epigraphically prolific, Levantine groups stretching from Alicante to Narbonne (*ill. 94*).

Iberian scripts were widely used into the first century, and the system was adopted by the Celtiberians in the Ebro valley and central Mesetas to write a wholly different – and Indo-European – language, before they

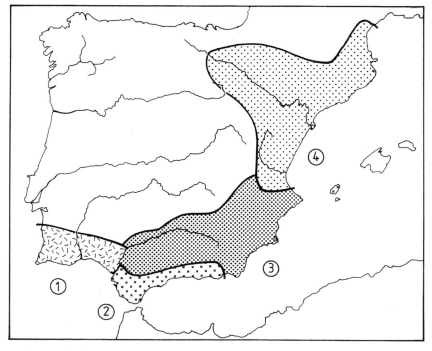

94 A map showing the distribution of the four main writing systems in the Iberian peninsula: *1* The southwestern script, *2* Phoenician, *3* Iberian script of Baetica, *4* Levantine script of the Iberians.

finally accepted the use of Latin at the change of the era. For most archaeologists, the uses of writing and the deductions one can make from the fact of provisional, or semi-literacy are nearly as interesting as the content of the written messages themselves, and the deft studies of Javier de Hoz make stimulating reading; they form the core of this discussion.

The southwest script was used in much the same manner as the early Phoenician, from which it derived; that is, for making ownership marks on pottery in the form of graffiti scratched on to the surface and for funerary inscriptions, cut into stone, and set above prominent graves so as to be visible to everyone who passed by. Both of these uses of a script are functional and obvious, just the things to be copied by semi-literate observers; parents of small children would notice a similar practice in their offspring. The more sophisticated writing for commerce and, perhaps, politics, would be concealed, and hence not easily copied. The most public Phoenician writing would be the inscribed pillars at the Herakleion outside Gadir. The southwest script, once its design was achieved, was enthusiastically applied to grave stelas, continuing a tradition of funerary magnificence already 700-years-old in the region (*ills. 95, 97*). The earlier Bronze Age monuments show only the dead person as a matchstick figure, surrounded by his chariot and arms; crude as they are, they are replaced by similarly rough and terse inscriptions, at a date widely believed to be around 600 BC. A fine stela from Abóbada (Portugal) marks the transition from one style to the other (*ill. 96*). These are restricted uses of writing. There are none of the practice alphabets, or public inscriptions and boundary markers, nor the slightest hint of any

301

305

308

95–97 **Language of stelas** (*Left*) An engraved stone stela from Fonte Velha, Bensafrím in the Algarve (Portugal), with an inscription written in the language of the southwest. (*Below, left and right*) The inscribed and decorated stone stela from Abóbada (Almodôvar) (Alemtejo, Portugal) is unique, since it combines the older style of depicting stick men with the later fashion for inscriptions in the language of the southwest. Its date is about 650 BC. (*Above*) Transcriptions from three more of the stelas in the southwest, which must be read from right to left. Nos. 301 and 305 from Fonte Velha (Bensafrím, Algarve). Stela 308 is also from the Algarve, but its exact findspot is unknown.

literary compositions being committed to permanent record by writing, as occurred in Etruria. Indeed, Classical writers specifically speak of the rich *oral* literature of the peoples of southern Spain, which survived until the Roman conquest, esteemed for its beauty and antiquity. But none of this, not a single poem, story, myth, or augury was written down and fixed for posterity. The use of script for a limited range of duties is a Phoenician habit; the Greeks early on used their writing skills far more imaginatively for every literary purpose, foremost among them being the preservation of their epic poetry.

Some disconcerting puzzles about the origins of the oldest script remain. For instance, if the script was derived from Phoenician, why was there a change from the thirty-two alphabetic characters used by the Phoenicians to a semi-syllabic one of only twenty-eight signs? And if the script was used by the Tartessians, how did it come to pass that all the finest inscriptions are found in southern Portugal rather than in the Guadalquivir valley and Huelva, the heartlands of Tartessos?

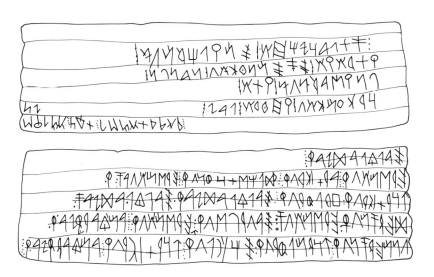

98 A letter written on lead strip in the Levantine Iberian alphabet from the village of La Bastida de les Alcuses (Mogente, Valencia). It bears three messages, which are transliterated below; their meaning is unknown. It was written about 300 BC.

Text 1:
... *skolibe : oduta : biśibetarakar*

Text 2:
*otalaugititebe : sikoltiŕikan :*
*kotarbekobe : sosinkukebeka : nanbin :*
*binkośaŕnkan : kotabe :*
*urkekuikebeka : kotekurbe : lagi :*

Text 3:
*şaldulakogiaŕ*
*erşibekaŕ : artakerkaŕ : akoltiśtautenkaŕ : ersibekau : ŕ*
*üortakerkaŕ : burlterkaŕ : şaldulakogiaŕ : şaldulakogiau :*
*koeruikaŕ : erşibekau : şakarbiskaŕ : erşibekaŕ : aiduarbegiaŕ :*
*kanieronkaŕ : üorilterkaŕ : stikelkaŕ : üortakerkaŕ : aiduarbegiaŕ :*

The southern Iberian script, or southeastern as it is sometimes called, is more widespread but still little known. Although it hides a different language from that used in the southwest, it is probably close to, or identical with, that which was written in the Levantine script. Our oldest, and longest, inscription is upon a lead sheet from the small town of La Bastida de les Alcuses (Mogente, Valencia), excavated from a house where it had been left behind once the place was destroyed around 300 BC (*ill. 98*). Other important pieces include the lead plaque found in 1862 in a mine at Gador (Almeria), which has the signs of a private document too, with lines ruled across it and three bookkeeping entries followed by numbers, as if quantities of products (or people) were being added. This is obviously a late piece of writing, since it includes latinisms in the text such as *Ego*, *tui* and *tecus*. The suite of silver tableware found at Abengibre (Albacete) has nine separate inscriptions hurriedly scratched on to some of the pieces, as if the owner(s) had scribbled their names so they could identify their silverplate later on.

Levantine script is the classical Iberian writing, with the most abundant documentation (*ill. 99*). The first examples date from 425 BC, with a Greek wine cup from Ullastret bearing its owner's name scratched in Iberian characters on the base. Its use expands greatly after 300 BC, as does its use in commerce; here the stimulus came from Greek traders at Emporion who must have shown its value to the Indikete people living next to them at Ullastret. Extensive use of mercenary soldiers in the Sicilian wars would be another occasion for acquiring ideas. The emphasis here, as in the southwest, is upon the use of writing by individuals rather than by the community. It is individual chiefs who have engraved stelas; rich men who want to put their names on fine pottery, and their names and bullion weight on their silver tableware; and individual merchants who need accounts for their commercial dealings in permanent form. With Romanization there was a notable change in this habit. Wholesale reorganization of the Iberian communities into new administrative forms persuaded the community to make use of writing, rather than leave it in the hands of selected individuals.

| | | | | | |
|---|---|---|---|---|---|
| Ɒ P P Ⴣ | A | Ν Ν | N | ϴ ① ⊗ ◊ ⊟ | DE,TE |
| Ⴣ Ⴣ Ⴣ ∧Ⴣ⌄ | E | ⎨ ⎨ ⎨ | S' | Ѱ Ψ Ψ Ψ | DI,TI |
| Ν Ν Ν | I | Μ Μ | S(Sh?) | Ⱳ Ⱳ Ⱳ | TO |
| Η Η Η Ν | O | I | BA | △ △ △ | DU,TU |
| ↑ ∧ | U | Ѫ Ѫ Ѫ Ѫ Ѯ | BE | ∧ ∧ ∩ ∩ | KA |
| Ⴣ ∧ | L | Γ Ρ | BI | ⟨ ⟨ ⟨ ℂ ℂ Ⴚ ℂ | KE |
| ◁ ◁ ◁ Я | R | ✕ ✕ ✕ | BO,PO,HO | ⟋ ⟋ ⟋ S ∧ | KI,GI |
| φ φ φ ♦ ◇ | R' | ▢ ⊡ | BU | ✕ ✕ ✕ ✕ | KO,GO |
| ∨ Y ⟨ T Ѱ Ⴣ | M,N | ✕ | DA,TA | ⊙ ○ ◇ | KU |

99 Letters used in the Levantine Iberian alphabet, with some of the more important variations. Modern sound equivalents are given on the right-hand side.

100 This letter written on a strip of lead using the Levantine Iberian alphabet, was found in the city of Ullastret (Gerona), in 1967. Its transcription is given below, although its meaning is unknown.

Inner text:
*Ar.basiaŕebe | ebaŕikame : tuikesiŕa : borste : abaŕkeborste : teŕ ... |*
*tiŕs : baidesbi : neitekeru : boŕbelioŕku : timoŕ ... | giŕ : bartasko :*
*anbeiku : baidesir : salduko kuleboberʹkuke bigiltiŕste : eŕeśu :*
*kotobanen : eberga : bośkalirs | loŕs : abatibi : biuŕbones :*
*saldugileŕku : n ...*

Outer text:
*taŕui : abobaker : abaśake : bosbeŕiun : erna : borakau :*

## Letters, inscriptions and graffiti

In the Greek world, personal notes, letters and commercial records were widely written on papyrus, and for that reason rarely survive, even though they were once common. The lead sheets used as writing material in the Spanish Levant were prepared specifically for use as a writing medium, an idea likely copied from the Greeks, who, in their remoter colonies far from supplies of cheap papyrus, had to devise another medium for letter writing, and appropriated malleable sheet lead for the purpose. Lead was always going to be common in seafaring towns, and is abundant all along the Spanish coasts.

As in the other regions, graffiti on pottery are far and away the commonest use for the script, especially on better quality Greek pottery. Most are personal names and ownership marks. The lead sheets seem to be a different class of document; about thirty survive. Some have a long inscription on one face, and a very short one upon the other, as if they were letters, with the recipient's address put on the outside. The pair of lead inscriptions from Ullastret were rolled up together in this manner,

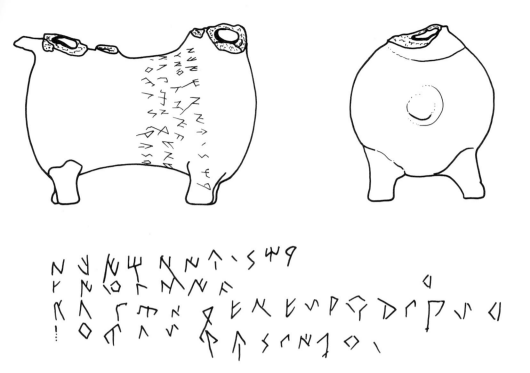

101 This hollow animal-shaped vessel of grey pottery (*rhyton*), bearing an inscription in the Levantine Iberian alphabet, is unique. It was discovered at Ullastret (Gerona) and was made in the fourth century BC.

Text:
*neitin iunstir | eigi kulnika ... r | belbitinko enegiaŕ aŕbigiŕ | aŕtingi ausŕikaŕ*

with the plainer one on the outside, its address visible to the bearer (*ill. 100*). Examples nearly as good were discovered by the excavators of the French *oppidum* at Pech Maho (Narbonne) who had the luck to find four lead letters (three of them still tightly rolled up) on the floor of a house in the commercial district of the Iberian town, and could date them between 225 and 200 BC. The domestic contexts of nearly all these inscriptions (the exception is the Graeco-Iberian lead from Grave 21 at Cigarralejo dated around 350 to 300 BC) reinforces their commercial aspect. The use of lead is likely to have been the normal material for letter writing and once scrapped, such letters could easily be remelted and recast into fresh writing material. The only other writing media for Levantine scripts are pottery, precious metal vessels (Tivissa), or stone (*ill. 101*).

Epigraphers have not been slow to notice a curious feature in these regional scripts; those in the south and southwestern areas are written in retrograde manner, from right to left; yet in the Levant and Catalonia, the reverse is true, and nearly all of them are written from left to right. This applies equally to lead and pottery texts. Exactly why this should be so is unclear.

Of all the sites with inscriptions painted upon pottery, that of the Cerro de San Miguel at Liria (Valencia) has the best collection. The words apparently describe the animated scenes and fights of which they form part; others are likely to be the painter's name. Their date is anywhere from the late third century to 76 BC, when the place was razed by the Romans. The few stone inscriptions, some of them grave stelas, concentrate around Emporion, Tarraco and Sagunto; most date to the period after the Roman conquest; there are no public inscriptions at all.

Dating this Levantine script depends upon the date of the pottery upon which it was engraved or painted. Thus, we know certainly that Iberian writing was used around 425 to 400 BC, and that the script developed in the southwest several centuries earlier.

After the Roman conquest there is a marked change in the frequency and use of Iberian writing. It is now used for coin legends issued by a plethora of mints all over the Iberian world. The Celtiberians, who only adopted coinage and writing in the middle of the second century, had rather different uses for it than their Iberian neighbours formerly had; not for graffiti and the like, but for public inscriptions such as the safe conduct passes and hospitality documents (the *tesserae hospitales*), and bronze tablets for display on buildings, as well as coins. This use of writing is communal rather than personal and particular. It is to display public rites, treaties, statuses and so forth for everyone's understanding, or at least, cognizance. All this shows that the needs of the Roman administration wrought a profound change in the writing habits and literary needs among the Iberian peoples, but even then it is doubtful if the culture as a whole could be described as possessing more than conditional literacy.

Iberians also experimented with other alphabets. There are a few inscriptions from Murcia and Alicante around 350 to 300 BC using the simplified Ionian Greek alphabet reduced to sixteen characters, to write the Iberian language. It proved too cumbersome and was inadequate. Later examples come from the open-air sanctuary at Villastar (Teruel) where the Latin alphabet was used for writing Celtiberian, and at the town of Botorrita (Zaragoza) a large tablet was inscribed with Iberian characters but using the Celtiberian language; it dates to about 90 BC.

It must not be forgotten that Iberia was home to many different written languages even in the sixth century BC; Semitic, Greek, Iberian, and after 218 BC, Latin too. The truly surprising thing is that so much writing has come down to us, and how rapidly the stock is increasing. There must be a rosy future beckoning epigraphists, although whatever is discovered is unlikely to fulfil Emile Durkheim's elevated hopes for '... priceless instruments of thought which human groups have laboriously forged through the centuries and where they have accumulated the best of their intellectual capital' (*The Elementary Forms of Religious Life*, 1915).

# 11 · Fruits of the earth: mining, farming and manufacturing

MINING AND AGRICULTURE are two promising areas to study where new work has enlightened us in some unexpected ways. The most radical reappraisal concerns the silver mines of the Río Tinto, a magnet for the Phoenicians from their earliest voyages, and the reason for the precocious orientalizing of the southwest. About agriculture we remain less well informed than we should like, but have made an excellent beginning.

## The silver mines of the Río Tinto

Behind the city of Huelva lie the famous mines of the Río Tinto, which are among the oldest workings in the world still in operation. They have disgorged an immense fortune in silver and copper for over 3000 years. Their exploitation goes far back into prehistory, with a notable peak of production at the time of the earliest Phoenician colonization of Iberia from the eighth to the sixth centuries. They are the reason for the prompt development of the southwest after 750 BC.

Running in a wide band across the southwest corner of Spain and Portugal for more than 100 km are mineral lodes rich in silver and copper, many peppered with old workings. Some mines have been dated to the Early Bronze Age in the first part of the second millennium and belong to indigenous, prehistoric industires, but the Río Tinto deposits completely dwarf them in size and richness.

Modern work on the antiquity and production of the Río Tinto mines has taken our knowledge far beyond what was known only a decade ago, thanks to the project of Beno Rothenberg and Antonio Blanco Freijeiro. It set itself two simple questions to answer: what metals were produced at these mines? and when did this production take place? Questions about the mechanics of metal production were left for a later stage of the project, which continues. The answers to these deceptively simple problems only make sense if we start at the beginning of the story.

The Río Tinto's name comes from its strange red colour, literally the 'dyed river' in Spanish; anyone who is sufficiently curious to see where it rises can easily do so, and trace it from the sea directly to the ore lodes in less than two days' walk. The livid hue comes from the iron salts which have leached out of the main ore bodies, and poison the river for its entire course.

The original topography of the mining area around the Río Tinto is now wholly altered from its primitive state. The old mining remains themselves have been obliterated largely by the modern open-cast works which have gouged whole mountains apart. Nevertheless, the scrappy traces of the oldest workings have been forced to reveal some of their secrets, and archaeological and metallurgical evidence agrees closely on the major points, proving that these mines were extracting silver from the soft jarositic ores before 800 BC. Millions of tons of rich ores were dug out from prehistoric to Roman times, and the slag heaps from these colossal enterprises are the largest known from any ancient mining works. Truly a vast investment of human effort and energy was devoted to them, and the wealth generated must have been in equally huge proportion.

It is known beyond doubt that silver was the chief metal produced at the Río Tinto until Roman times. The silver slag heaps generally lie apart from the slags left behind from copper smelting which took place later under the Romans. The volumes of these slags had been nearly impossible to estimate accurately, but a detailed survey by Rothenberg's team has shown that the figure of 6,000,000 tons is much closer to the truth than the old estimates of over 16,000,000; furthermore, most of the slag is from smelting silver ores (*ill. 102*). Much of it has been covered over, or quarried away, or used as ballast on the 86 km of railway track linking the mines with the port of Huelva, but important residues survived for study. Originally, the main body of these slags extended over an area 1.5 km long, 0.5 km wide, with an average thickness of 6 m.

The mineral bodies from which the ores were dug comprise a thick mantle of gossan (*ill. 103*), orginally up to 30 m in depth, covering a massive sulphide deposit (gossan is the cap on an ore deposit formed of rust-coloured oxides, with a preponderance of iron and lesser amounts of silver, gold and other minerals). Where the two met lay a zone of secondary mineral enrichment, at the base of the gossan, which held the silver ores. These were brightly coloured earths of yellow, red, grey, and black layers classified as argentiferous jarosites; rare minerals of predominantly yellow–brown colour with a brilliant lustre, composed of iron, hydrous potassium and aluminium sulphate with irregular quantities of silver minerals. Directly beneath them lie the layers enriched with copper, which only began to be mined in the first century AD. Other metals existed too: gold, arsenic, antimony, and lead. Today, none of the silver-rich jarositic earths are left, and hardly any were left in 1887, when the last pocket of 30,000 tons was mined. This means that the original richness cannot be assayed exactly, but the samples from the pocket showed that the silver content was extremely variable, from 3.1 kg per ton of ore to nothing at all. Figures as high as 10 kg per ton could well have occurred in the richest spots. These assays are extraordinarily high and compare with modern ones which consider 0.6 kg of silver per ton to be among the richest still being mined today.

The ancient mine workings were recorded summarily before they disappeared, but fortunately some have survived to be surveyed and

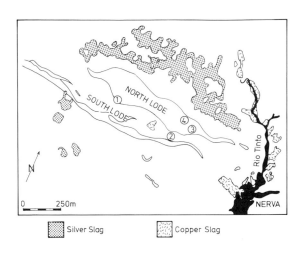

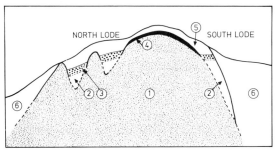

102, 103 **Mining in the Río Tinto** (*Right, above*) A simplified plan of the ore lodes and archaeological sites at the Río Tinto mines in Huelva. The extent of the slag heaps from silver and copper working is shown. The numbers indicate the following sites: *1* Cerro Colorado; *2* Cerro Salomón; *3* Quebrantahuesos; *4* Corta Lago. (*Right, below*) A schematic geological section of Río Tinto to show the location of the silver ore lodes. The numbers indicate the following strata: *1* Volcanic rocks; *2* massive sulphides; *3* gossan and secondary sulphides 30 m thick, rich in copper, silver and gold; *4* lower zone of the gossan, 3 m thick and rich in silver, gold, and with a little copper; *5* gossan from massive sulphides; *6* slates.

excavated. They include simple 'cave mines', as well as shafts with galleries off them; such tunnels have been located directly below the Tartessian settlement on the hill of Quebrantahuesos. Old photographs from around 1880, and descriptions made by the Spanish priest Diego Delgado in 1556–57 corroborate modern observations.

Some of the key places where the prehistoric activity of the mines could be studied were the two native settlements of Cerro Salomón and Quebrantahuesos, and the stratified slag heap at the Corta Lago, at the foot of the Cerro Salomón. The dominating hill in the locality is the Cerro Salomón, with fresh water springs at its base. The main settlement was on top; it was a small affair, and although it may have linked up with the village of Quebrantahuesos on a nearby hill, there is nothing to prove that it did. Scattered traces of buildings of various dates down to the Arab period, and Roman industrial structures, extend over the entire length of the hill, a distance of some 900 m. Little of this was studied before it was quarried away in the 1970s, but excavations in 1966–7 found houses dated by the imported Phoenician pottery in them to 725–550 BC. There was later pottery too, including the foot from a Greek wine cup made in Attica, which fixes a date in the fourth century. The settlement was of flimsy, rectangular buildings with adjoining rooms of the same size, resting on foundations of slate and floored with beaten earth. Inside the houses were obvious traces of metal-working; granite pestles and mortars, silver-rich slags, lead droplets, and fragments of clay nozzles from bellows used to heat the furnaces up to the required temperatures. The slags still contained up to 0.6 kg of silver per ton, which confirms that silver was being obtained and refined here, and that a very rich silver ore was mined. The lead droplets within the houses show that silver was extracted by adding lead and cupellating the mixture. Lead isotope analysis from the slags at Corta Lago shows that the lead from Tartessian layers was local Río Tinto metal; but after the third century this supply was insufficient, and imported lead was required to keep up the rate of silver production.

The smelting of the ores actually took place away from the settlement, down in the valleys opposite the mines. This is both more efficient and would have kept the stifling pollution away from the immediate vicinity of the village. But the cupellation of silver, where the lead is added to the furnace to join with the silver, and is then oxidized away with a strong blast of air to leave a button of silver metal behind, would have created clouds of poisonous fumes of lead oxide. The settlement must have been constantly tainted with noxious gases, smoke, and waste from the industrial operations all around, and a thoroughly disagreeable place to live.

Details of the miners' lives can be gleaned from their houses. They obtained olive oil and wine, since Phoenician amphoras for these products are common. They also had a few lamps of good quality imported types, but the commonest pottery was handmade, not made on a fast potter's wheel in the Phoenician manner, which suggests strongly that the inhabitants of these mining shacks were not Phoenicians but local people, who worked the mines directly, and imported a few Phoenician foodstuffs and utensils. A contingent of a few hundred is all that can be documented as composing the workforce for the mining and smelting operations. Nothing is known of the diet of these miners, or about their health, or longevity. We do not even know if their families lived with them on the Cerro Salomón. It would be fascinating to see if the abundant industrial pollution injured the miners' health, or not; it probably did. It is also suspected that all the food consumed would have to be brought into the mines, since the immediate area is agriculturally barren and will not grow cereals, which were the staple food. Supplying even a modest sized community with the basic necessities of life would have been a big job, and probably a centralized one; mining is essentially a collective endeavour. The mining force at Río Tinto, plus another one growing food surpluses and keeping bulk transport to feed them, with yet more at work felling timber and roasting charcoal for the furnaces, adds up to a substantial number of people directly employed in the operations. If the mines were worked seasonally, for a short period each year, and the miners doubled up as farmers and lumbermen when not digging

104 View of Corta Lago with slag formations above the uppermost step of the open-cast mine. Tartessian silver slags lie at the base, dated to the eighth century BC.

minerals, then the production would be much smaller. It is precisely the large scale of the works that compels us to think in large numbers of permanent miners.

On the north slope of the Cerro Salomón lies the Cueva del Lago, the (legendary) source of the Río Tinto, whose vitriolic waters are even here stained deep red. Nearby on the northeast side of the Cerro Salomón, lies the Corta Lago slag heap, and a section over 500 m long and nearly 8 m high was exposed by modern mining in the early years of this century (*ill. 104*). This sequence is being analysed in great detail by Rothenberg's team, and proves to be composed of many separate metallurgical working surfaces, formed by dumps of slag, each one from a single run of a furnace. Only in the uppermost levels, belonging to the imperial Roman workings, did very large slag tips appear. The lowest levels were of the late Bronze Age, succeeded by the Tartessian, Iberian and Punic ones. Even the prehistoric slags show that silver extraction was a well organized business, not a cottage industry; the slags from the oldest levels were all properly tapped from stone furnaces lined with clay, and mixed in with them were thick crucible-, or cupel-, fragments, for holding liquid metal or cupellating silver. The slags were analysed from each of the hundred or more layers up to the Roman period, and were shown to be nearly all lead-silver ones. These tests were repeated right up to the Roman slag layers, where copper, and possibly a little iron, was found. The iron production was only on a small scale for the manufacture of tools for use in the mines, while the copper grew into a real source of wealth for the Romans, and was remarked upon by Pliny in the first century AD.

One long-standing mystery about the metal content of the slags was solved recently. The slags have less than 1 per cent of lead or copper in them, compared to values as high as 17 per cent or 30 per cent elsewhere in the ancient world. This feature was not due to a secret, efficient smelting technique that died with the Romans, but to a leaching of the silver, gold and copper out of the slags by rainwater, and the redeposition of these metals 2 to 4 m below the slag piles, in the uppermost layer of bedrock. The copper, being more soluble in water, migrated to greater depths.

The origins of the silver smelting technology are not clear. The discovery of a Bronze Age cemetery of stone cists at Río Tinto in 1981 led to the more important find in their immediate vicinity of a pit filled with Bronze Age pottery, nodular slag, and a clay crucible with traces of silver inside it. This confirms that silver production was already under-way at Río Tinto *before* the arrival of Phoenician colonists in Spain, and that the technology was not introduced through their agency. The fact that this technology is fully prehistoric is significant, since there must be a developmental sequence in the region to account for it, but for the moment it remains hidden from view. The scale of mining and smelting in the eighth to the seventh centuries was modest compared to the huge scale of the Roman works, and still in the hands of the local people. The small quantities of Phoenician artefacts on the site do not indicate the physical presence of Phoenicians at the mines; indeed, in their homeland they had no mines, or technological expertise in mining to transmit to others, so their presence at the Río Tinto would be odd indeed. Their role was always that of traders and manufacturers of specialities, not delvers for metals.

Besides the mines themselves, one has to consider the fuel needed to stoke the furnaces. Most of this came from oak wood, using the local evergreen oaks (encinas; *Quercus ilex*) for charcoal. Consumption has been quantified by mining engineers whose figures make sober reading. They show that about 100 kg of oak wood was needed to roast and smelt ores to yield 1 kg of copper, or 0.1 kg of silver; furthermore, the yield of an acre of woodland in the immediate vicinity of the mines would not be more than 93 tons in forty-three years, or less than 2 tons per acre each year. At this rate hundreds-of-thousands of tons of wood had to be found to smelt the ores, and probably swiftly deforested the surrounding region. More exact figures could be calculated for the fuel consumption if the volume of slag for each period was accurately known, but even very conservative estimates of slag tonnage, firing efficiency, and so on, still force one to accept that enormous volumes of fuel were needed at the Río Tinto mines, and would have to be supplied by a large workforce. This is yet another reason for thinking that the mines were worked on a substantial scale even in prehistoric times (*ill. 105*).

## Trade in silver bullion – a speculation

How much silver was produced in pre-Roman times? Where did it go? Reliable figures cannot be got for the first question, since the original

105 General view of the Cerro Colorado (Río Tinto, Huelva), with the mine works visible in the distance.

richness of the ores, and their volumes, are both unknown. Guesses are unlikely to be helpful. Whatever the true volume, it clearly amounted to metallic wealth on a great scale. Its destination is easier to consider.

The silver seems to have ended up pretty rapidly in the hands of Phoenician traders in southern Spain, probably those based in Gadir, since the graves of wealthy indigenes have very little of the metal. Its ultimate destination was far from Spain; in fact, there are excellent reasons for believing it was shipped by Phoenician trading families directly to Tyre or another Levantine port, and used to pay the tribute demanded from Phoenicia by her Assyrian masters. Assyrian resurgence in the late eighth century was due to Tiglath-Pileser's destruction of the North Syrian and Urartian powers to the north and west of his empire; to the south and southwest he was able to make vassals of Israel and Judah.

Only the Phoenician cities retained their independence, a status permitted to them so long as they were the main suppliers of primary raw materials to Assyria. This new role for the Phoenicians required them to expand their trade farther afield than ever before, and on a scale hitherto unknown. They did this by setting up new manufactories for finished goods, which could then be exchanged for the raw materials which were demanded from them. At the same time the value of all goods circulating in Assyria became assessible against a fixed standard of silver metal. By the reign of Sargon in the late seventh century, the supply of silver had increased so sharply that it was used throughout the empire as the accepted currency, and may actually have declined in value. All this can be linked plausibly to the success of the Phoenicians in locating and exploiting the Río Tinto silver mines in the late eighth century, and most especially to the establishment of firmer control over the Phoenician cities after the fall of Sidon to King Esarhaddon in 671 BC. One direct consequence would be demands for extra tribute, which could be met with Spanish silver. If this reconstruction is broadly correct, it serves to explain the inflow of silver to Assyria, the Phoenician role as middlemen, and gives an acceptable date in the seventh century for the main exploitation of the Río Tinto lodes. The scale of silver production seems to have filled the Assyrian coffers to overflowing.

Other places in southern Spain were also mining and producing silver in the seventh century, and for many hundreds of years afterwards. The mines at Cástulo, near the city of Linares (Jaén) were of great wealth, and excavations at the orientalizing settlement of Baños de la Muela near Cástulo itself found silver-rich slags. In the port of Huelva, upon the steep hills within the modern city, other orientalizing settlements have been unearthed, and had silver slags and crucibles too. Phoenician pottery and other commodities are common at the sites of the Cabezo de San Pedro and La Esperanza, and the grave goods of the princely dead in the cemetery of La Joya date back to 650 BC. The height of the Phoenician trade with their homeland was in this century, and is attested at the best known of all their colonies in Spain, Toscanos, where relations were intensest in the seventh century.

## Agriculture

Most studies of Iberian agriculture prefer to cite Classical writers like Strabo, Pliny and Varro rather than obtain direct information at firsthand. Secondary or tertiary sources like these describe conditions as they were in the last century BC, when Iberia was well under Roman control, and large areas of Andalusia had been organized for olive oil production. They are of limited use for earlier periods, and contain factual errors; nevertheless, direct evidence for farming has been sadly neglected.

Our point of departure is not from Classical texts but from plants and tools used in farming. We know that later Bronze Age agriculture was based on growing hard wheat and barley, and raising all the major domestic animals; cattle, sheep, pig, and horse. Certain sites already specialized in livestock trade with their neighbours. Of lesser importance were crops like flax, beans, and vetches, grown perhaps to intercrop with the cereals to keep the land fertile. Wild foods were collected from woodlands and meadows; wild olives, and grapes, as well as acorns, were all eaten by 3000 BC. This is an agriculture which is essentially western European. It emphasizes cereal production, and lacks the key elements that we think of today as Mediterranean, and which dominate whole provinces in Spain: olives for oil, and grapes for wine. At some time between 800 BC, when our documentation for late Bronze Age farming ceases, and 500–450 BC, when it begins for Iberian agriculture, there is an expansion or enlargement whereby olives and vines begin to be grown, as well as fruit trees like pomegranates, figs, and dates. The manufacture of clay amphoras suitable for holding olive oil or wine began about 550 BC;

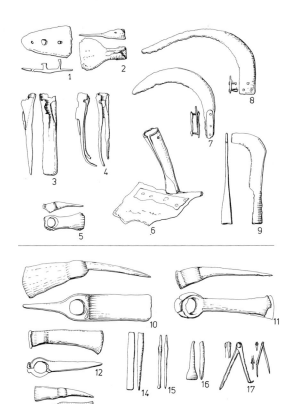

106–107 **Tools from La Bastida de les Alcuses (Mogente, Valencia)**
(*Above*) Agricultural tools made of wrought iron, including: *1* ploughshare; *2* end of paddle staff to knock clods of soil off the ploughshare; *3* laya, or narrow spade, for deep digging; *4* laya for deep digging in hard soil; *5* weed hook or small hoe; *6* large digging hoe for work in soft soil; *7* light sickle; *8* scythe; *9* socketed billhook. (*Below*) Wrought-iron tools for woodworking and other crafts, including: *10* heavy axe-mattock; *11* socketed adze; *12* axe with a blunt back; *13* small axe-adze or 'picoleta'; *14* chisel; *15* drill bit; *16* paring chisel for fine work; *17* compass; *18* broken-legged compass; *19* saw; *20* spring shears; *21* leather-cutting knife; *22* knife for splitting or paring leather; *23* esparto sewing needle; *24* curved knife with tang for its wooden haft, *25* small cleaver with hole for suspension. All these tools date to around 300 BC.

they are wheel-turned vessels of good enough quality to stop the products inside from turning rancid with oxidation. Direct evidence in the form of olive presses with pits, or grape pips in dumps near a winery have not been found yet; olive pollen does appear in levels of peat in the coastal marshes of Huelva around 600 BC, however. Something nearly as good are the specialized iron tools used to prune fruit trees; prepare slits for grafting new varieties on to local root stocks; dig deep, narrow pits for the initial planting.

The village of La Bastida in Valencia again comes to our aid with the best collection of Iberian farming implements, along with an elegant discussion of their uses by Enrique Pla Ballester (*ills. 106, 107*). From them it is clear that extensive dry farming with light ploughs was practised, and that cereals were grown abundantly, as in the later Bronze Age. Such farming requires draught animals like oxen to be effective. Then there are the tools especially for working in loose, moist soil such as we find in irrigated plots or market gardens. These are for hand labour

108 Shapes of Iberian pottery made between 500 and 200 BC. The group on the left illustrates forms wholly indigenous to Spain; the group on the right is of pottery locally made, copying Greek shapes.

and intensive gardening. Large hoes and narrow-bladed spades are the tools for this work; weeding could be done with a light weed hook. Most of these tools are unusuable in dry farming; they would not last a month without buckling in the hard earth. We do not know how extensive irrigation was, or if it was formalized in any way with channels and canals. It was probably confined strictly to river bottoms where a little work making temporary dykes would be sufficient to divert water profitably to neighbouring fields. Irrigation with substantial water works belongs to the Roman period.

The curved knives, socketed billhooks, light and heavy axes and adzes are all tools apt for pruning trees or vines, and the axe-adzes would be suitable for general woodworking too. All of these things date to around 300 BC. The question is, how far back in time does their use go? There is nothing remotely like this selection of well adapted and ingeniously designed tools in the Bronze Age; indeed, metal was too scarce for farming implements, so flint was used instead. The obvious sources for the tools, and for the crops with which they are connected, are the Phoenicians. The intensely competitive orientalizing period must surely have awoken interest in the plants that could produce the oil and wine that were so much liked, just as mining silver expanded. It is probable that the grafts and root-stocks were brought from colonial enclaves and transplanted inland, since the native varieties were unsuitable, and neither olives nor vines breed well from their seeds; they tend to revert to coarser types. In this way production spread inland. If the amphoras were manufactured locally, are correctly dated to the sixth century, and could be analysed for oil or wine residues, then we could support better the idea that the shift towards a Mediterranean pattern of production was well under-way by then. Interest in the new crops does not mean that stock raising and cereal growing were neglected; far from it, they remained as they do to this day, the staple foods of the country. Olives and vines require more hand labour than cereals, or livestock, and as they become more important in the Iberian economy, so too would more labour be needed on the farms. If there was a population increase from the sixth to the third centuries, then these crops would be one manner in which profitable work could be found for it.

## Manufactures

The perishable nature of so many everyday products, especially textiles and wood, has deprived us of countless treasures. The tools from La Bastida include sprung shears for clipping wool, and a complete set of carpentry tools. Better fortune attended the excavator of the rich graves in the cemetery at Cigarralejo (Murcia) because he located remains of fancy wooden boxes and turned bowls with lids made in boxwood. Fragments of other woods showed more than usual skill in selection; poplar, lime, ash, olive, pine and laurel had all been used by the craftsmen. These graves had Greek pottery of the fourth century, so they are roughly contemporary with the village of La Bastida. Carbonized wooden furniture inlaid with engraved bone strips was found at Cancho Roano (Badajoz), and although its forms are unknown, it was intricately carved with pleasing geometric designs in high relief; some pieces were ornamented with cast bronze figurines. It was perhaps a piece such as a 'bargueño' or ornamental chest of drawers on a stand; it too dates to the fourth century.

Ironworking technology was brought by the Phoenicians. At their colony of Toscanos iron slags and clay nozzles for heating the forge were discovered in levels associated with the use of the 'counting house' around 700 BC. Iron objects of Phoenician design such as long curved knives with ivory and silver handles were found in orientalizing graves at La Joya (Huelva), and Phoenician ones at Almuñécar. Iron was still treated as a rare commodity. The oldest iron swords are faithful copies of bronze ones, like the broken blade from a grave at Estacar de Robarinas (Cástulo) (*ill. 13, no. 1*). Iberian communities had knowledge of iron from the seventh century, and began to make extensive use of it for agricultural tools from the fifth century onwards. Swords of wrought iron, chased with silver, were found in the last century at Almedinilla (Cordoba), and their superb forging and decoration show how able blacksmiths had become by the fifth and fourth centuries. The shapes of these weapons copy the Greek sabre, and were sharpened both sides of the point to allow a slashing blow to be made while recovering a stroke.

Pottery production was revolutionized by the introduction of the fast potter's wheel. The oldest pottery made in this manner is from the colonial sites, and some is undoubtedly imported from Phoenicia and Greece. Local manufacture of the type called 'grey ware' starts before 700 BC; it is found on all Phoenician and Greek sites in Spain, and after 600 BC, production of a strikingly similar pottery is under-way in Catalonia. Local copies are many, and start early, since the clays used in making this pottery have all sorts of different mineral inclusions in them. It was used for a great range of bowls and plates. A contrasting type of pottery was 'red-polished ware', also a Phoenician idea, starting in the eighth century in Iberia, which lasted until about 450 BC. Its colours were lovely deep

109–111 **Pottery from Elche (Alicante)** (*Above, left*) A *kalathos* or hat-shaped pot, decorated with a fierce bird of prey. This is a motif which occurs time and again on fine pottery from this region. (*Above, right, top*) Detail of a *carnassier* or carnivorous beast painted on an Iberian pot. Note the excellence of the figure painting and the stylized plant motifs which fill the space within the design. (*Above, right*) Detail of a scene painted on an Iberian *pithos*. A cloaked and hooded man (with a stubbly chin) leads a saddled horse. The bird of prey and plant motifs again recur, as on other vessels from this region. All these pieces were made in the second century BC.

reds, corals, and oranges, usually with a burnished surface to give it a lustre. The colour can be applied all over, or just inside, or only around the rim. Nor is it an homogeneous class; like the grey ware, it had many kiln sites. Iberian potters adopted this style between 450 and 300 BC, although their firings gave a more purple or brown hue to the colour. Forms are varied, and the Phoenician forms popular in the east are mostly the ones maintained in the west; indigenous wares have different shapes (*ill. 108*).

Painted decoration was popular a little later, again starting as a Semitic idea around 700 BC, then being picked up by native potters. It is often hard to separate painted from red-polished ware when only part of the surface has been burnished. Designs start with simple horizontal lines or red paint of infinitely varied thicknesses and arrangements applied with a multiple brush. They give way gradually to big concentric circles around 600 BC, then to smaller patterns of multiple arcs, bullseyes, parallel festoons, and fans. It is simple but effective decoration that is attractive to modern taste.

These fashions begin in western Andalusia by 600 BC, becoming commonest between 500 and 400 BC; they spread rapidly eastwards as far as Murcia by 600–550 BC. This geometric ornament was applied to all kinds of pottery: amphoras, plates, bowls, deep jars, and so on. Its popularity faded after 400 BC, but never died out altogether. Plant or vegetal motifs enter the repertoire next in the fourth century, used in lively registers or enlarged to fill the rounded volume of the vase. But the most spectacular figured vases, the ones with lively scenes and even Iberian writing, are later still. Creative centres of outstanding quality arose at Elche and Archena, with wonderful stylized carnivores (*ills. 109–11*); at Liria (Valencia) with a baroque style all of its own (*ill. 112*), every pot an individual piece; and at Azaila (Teruel), where animated scenes in a silhouette style show men and dramas of great vigour. Pottery like this was made between 200 and 50 BC, in the 'Baja Epoca' of the Iberian world, just as it was being Romanized steadily and remorselessly. As a cultural or artistic achievement it has a barbaric confidence that successfully conceals the message it contains. What are the scenes depicted? Some are rituals, others legends and stories, others just jolly ornament. We cannot say when such splendid pottery was used, or by whom; civic functions, funerary cults, ordinary profane uses all come to mind. When we can penetrate this symbolic world of the Iberian imagination, we shall have a properly intimate understanding of these societies. For the time being, we can only admire, describe, and date it.

112 The 'warrior vase' from the Iberian town of Liria (Valencia), destroyed in 76 BC. Some believe the scene is a dance, perhaps at a funeral, and that the rosettes and stylized 'lizards' are religious symbols.

# Epilogue

SCIPIO'S ENTRY into the Greek colony of Emporion in 218 BC at the start of the Second Punic War marks the end of Iberian independence; the heavy fighting in that war, the ensuing rebellion of the Iberian towns in Andalusia against Roman exactions from 195 BC; then the long series of wars first in the Ebro valley then on the Mesetas, forcibly assimilated the peninsula to Roman customs. It was systematic conquest totally distinct from the way in which influence was exercised from the old colonial stations; it progressively changed Iberian culture; its institutions, settlement patterns, art, all were bent to Rome's purposes. This is well-seen in the Ebro valley. Between 200 and 50 BC Iberian settlements were compacted stage by stage into ever larger and fewer units along the fertile river valleys. Then there are the scores of small towns in north Spain which were granted authority to mint their own bronze and silver coins under the Roman authorities, and indeed, many of them became urban for the first time under this new regime. Socially, the effect would have been homogenizing.

Iberia became less economically detached. It was drawn ever more tightly into the Mediterranean embrace, and all the signs of cash cropping in olives and vines are visible in Andalusia by 100 BC. After a long period of material poverty, caused by Carthaginian exactions, then the wars and rebellions marked archaeologically by several dozen hoards of silver scrap and tableware, something like prosperity returns late in the first century. The period between 237 and 49 BC was a time when huge wealth was drained from the country.

Literacy was now more widespread, and writing used in a different manner, for public documents such as the legal ones on bronze written in Latin and Celtiberian from Botorrita (Zaragoza), and on coins; these became so common, and there is so much small change in circulation after 133 BC, that it may well have had an economic effect of unlocking capital immobilized in agricultural assets, thereby promoting greater prosperity – or more tax revenue for Rome. The notable thing about the coinages is that they bear the names of *towns*, not tribes, like the Celtic coinages did in neighbouring Gaul. Iberian inscriptions were added to prominent funerary monuments.

Iberian culture found itself under relentless pressure as the pace of Romanization accelerated; this assimilation is what makes the 'Baja Epoca' qualitatively different from the older period of Iberian achievement, and its agents are Italic and Roman, not Semitic.

| DATES BC | HISTORICAL EVENTS IN THE EASTERN MEDITERRANEAN | CATALONIA, BALEARICS & SOUTHEAST SPAIN | ANDALUSIA |
|---|---|---|---|
| 1100 | | 1100–600 Late and Final Bronze Age groups related to the Urnfield cultures | 1100 traditional date for the founding of the city of Gadir |
| 1000 | 1025–880 zenith of Phoenician prosperity and independence | | 1000–800 Late and Final Bronze Age societies flourish |
| 900 | 969–936 Hiram, King of Tyre | | 900 Atlantic Bronze Age metalwork appears |
| | 883–859 Ashurnasirpal II subdues northern Syria and reaches the Mediterranean coast | | 850 Huelva board; elaborate grave stelas |
| 800 | 800 Greeks establish a trading station at Al Mina (Syria) | 800 Cerro de San Cristobál (Cabezo de Monleón) | 800–775 first Phoenician colonies set up on the Malaga coast |
| | 775 Greeks set up trading post on Ischia (Bay of Naples) | 750 gold hoard of Villena deposited | |
| 700 | 733 Greeks settle Syracuse | | 700–650 Phoenician colony at Toscanos prospering and expanding |
| | | | 650–600 Peak of Rio Tinto mines |
| | 671 Sidon captured by Esarhaddon | | 650–550 ORIENTALIZING PERIOD: |
| | | 654/3 Phoenicians colonize Ibiza | Huelva sites (La Joya cemetery) |
| 600 | 612 Assyrians defeated by the Babylonians | | Setefilla acropolis and cemetery |
| | | 600 Greeks found colony at Massilia | El Acebuchal cemetery Cults established at |
| | 573 Tyre surrenders to Nebuchadnezzar | 575 Greeks settle colonists at Emporion and Rhode | Despeñaperros |
| | | 550 Ullastret settled | 600–550 gold treasures like Carambolo and Lebrija |
| | 540 Persian conquest of Ionia | 550–450 ORIENTALIZING PERIOD in the Balearics | 550 towns now widespread in the interior of Andalusia |
| | | | 550–500 Iberian culture |
| 500 | | 500 Ullastret fortified | fully developed and spread |
| | 480 Xerxes defeated at Salamis | 500 monument at Pozo Moro built | into southwest France |
| | 431–404 Peloponnesian War | 450 Iberian script in use | 450 Cancho Roano built |
| | | | 450–400 Porcuna sculptures carved |
| 400 | | 400 Carthaginian trading posts set up in Mallorca | 450–350 climax of Iberian prosperity |
| | | 400–350 Tivissa fortified in the Greek style | 450–350 Carthaginian prosperity in Gadir, Sexi and |
| | 359 accession of Philip II of Macedon | 400–350 'Dama de Elche' carved | other colonies |
| | | 400–300 extensive destruction of towns and villages | 400–350 'Dama de Baza' buried |
| | | 375 Iberian expansion into the Ebro valley | |
| | | 340 El Sec shipwreck | |
| | 323 death of Alexander the Great | | |
| 300 | | 300 Iberian stone sculpture ceases in the southeast | |
| | | | 237 Carthaginian conquest of south Spain begins under Hamilcar Barca |
| | | 218 Hannibal captures Saguntum | 206 Romans capture Gadir and end the Carthaginian |
| 200 | | 217 Cato lands with Roman army at Emporion | occupation |

# Select Bibliography

This is a small list chosen for its quality, availability and cross-references to other published work. I have grouped books by chapter, and added a few comments where appropriate. Many specific subjects are discussed in the journals *Ampurias* (Barcelona), *Archivo Español de Arqueología* (Madrid) and *Madrider Mitteilungen* (Heidelberg).

## Introduction

ARRIBAS, A. *The Iberians*, London and New York, 1963.

BLAZQUEZ, J. M., F. PRESEDO, F. J. LOMAS and J. FERNANDEZ NIETO *História de España. Tomo I. Protohistoria* (2nd ed.), Madrid, 1983 [Valuable for its detail, but lacks form as a whole.]

BOSCH GIMPERA, P. *Etnología de la Península Ibérica*, Barcelona, 1932.

– *El Poblamiento Antiguo y la Formación de los Pueblos de España*, Mexico City, 1944 [elegantly designed and written books, well worth reading].

GARCIA Y BELLIDO, A. *Arte Ibérico en España*, Madrid, 1980.

HARDEN, D. *The Phoenicians*, London and New York, 1962 [still the best general text in English about the Phoenicians].

NICOLINI, G. *Les Iberes. Art et Civilization*, Paris, 1973.

SCHULTEN, A. *Tartessos*, Madrid, 1972 [Spanish translation of text last revised in 1944].

## 1 Spanish landscapes

HOUSTON, J. M. *The Western Mediterranean World*, London, 1964.

LAUTENSACH, H. *Iberische Halbinsel: Geographische Handbucher*, Munich, 1964.

RIPOLL PERELLO, E., M. LLONGUERAS CAMPAÑA, and E. SANMARTI I GREGO, (eds., *Simposio Internacional 'Els Origens del Mòn Ibèric'*, Barcelona-Ampurias 1977 (2 special volumes of *Ampurias*, Vols. 38–40), Barcelona, 1980.

SMITH, C. DELANO *Western Mediterranean Europe. A Historical Geography of Italy, Spain and Southern France since the Neolithic*, London, New York, Toronto, Sydney and San Francisco, 1979.

TERAN, M. de and L. SOLE SABARIS, eds., *Geografía Regional de España*, Barcelona, 1968.

## 2 The Bronze Age Mosaic

ALMAGRO BASCH, M. *Las Estelas Decoradas del Suroeste Peninsular*, Bibliotheca Praehistorica Hispana 8, Madrid, 1966.

BELTRAN MARTINEZ, A. Las casas del poblado de la I Edad del Hierro del Cabezo de Monleón (Caspe), *Boletín del Museo de Zaragoza* N° 3, 23–100, Zaragoza, 1984.

BLASCO BOSQUED, Mª. C. Un nuevo yacimiento del Bronce Madrileño; El Negralejo (Rivas-Vaciamadrid, Madrid). *Noticiario Arqueológico Hispánico* 17, 45–190, Madrid, 1983.

COFFYN, A. *Le Bronze Final Atlantique dans la Péninsule Ibérique*, Paris, 1985.

GIL MASCARELL, M. and C. ARANEGUI GASCO *El Bronce Final y el Comienzo de la Edad del Hierro en el Pais Valenciano*, Monografias del Laboratorio de Arqueología de Valencia N° 1, Valencia, 1981.

HARRISON, R. J. 'The "Policultivo Ganadero" or Secondary Products Revolution in Spanish Agriculture 5000–1000 BC', *Proceedings of the Prehistoric Society 51*, 75–102, 1985.

HARRISON, R. J. and P. CRADDOCK *A Study of the Bronze Age Metalwork from the Iberian Peninsula in the British Museum*. (Institut de Prehistoria i Arqueologia, Diputació de Barcelona. Monografia LXIV), Barcelona, 1983.

HARRISON, R. J., G. MORENO LOPEZ and A. J. LEGGE '*Moncín: Poblado Prehistórico de la Edad del Bronce (I)*'. *Noticiario Arqueológico Hispánico Vol. 28*, Madrid, 1988.

MOLINA GONZALEZ, F. Definición y sistematización del Bronce Tardío y Final en el Sudeste de la Península Ibérica. *Cuadernos de Prehistoria de la Universidad de Granada* ° *3*, 159–232, Granada, 1978.

SCHUBART, H. *Die Kultur der Bronzezeit im Südwesten der Iberischen Halbinsel.*

Madrider Forschungen Bd. 9, Berlin, 1975.

SOLER GARCIA, J. M. *El Tesoro de Villena*. Excavaciones Arqueológicas en España Vol. 36, Madrid, 1965.

## 3 Phoenician colonies

BARTOLONI, P., S. F. BONDI, G. C. POLSELLI, M. T. FRANCISI, F. MAZZA, G. PETRUCCIOLI and P. XELLA eds., *Atti del I Congresso Internatzionale di Studi Fenici e Punici* (Roma 5–10 Nov. 1978) 3 Vols., Rome, 1983.

BLAZQUEZ, J. M. *Tartessos y los Origenes de la Colonización Fenicia en Occidente* (2nd and revised ed), Salamanca, 1975. [indispensable, well-illustrated and thorough in its coverage].

BUNNENS, G. L'Expansion Phénicienne en Méditerranée. Essai d'interpretation fondé sur une analyse des traditions littéraires. *L'Institut Historique Belge de Rome, Vol. XVII* (Brussels and Rome), 1979).

FRANKENSTEIN, S. 'The Phoenicians in the Far West: a function of Neo-Assyrian imperialism', in M. T. LARSEN, ed., *Power and Propaganda. A Symposium on Ancient Empires*, 263–94, Copenhagen, 1979 [the finest and most succinct survey available on the relations between Phoenicians and their Assyrian neighbours].

GARCIA Y BELLIDO *Fenicios y Cartagineses en Occidente*, Madrid, 1942 [dated but with a wealth of useful detail].

MAAS-LINDEMANN, G. *Toscanos. Die Westphönikische Niederlassung an der Mündung des Río de Velez*. Madrider Forschungen Bd. 6.3, Berlin, 1982.

MOORE CROSS, F. Phoenicians in Sardinia: the Epigraphical Evidence. In: M. Balmuth and R. J. Rowland Jr, eds., *Studies in Sardinian Archaeology*, 53–65, Ann Arbor, Michigan, 1984.

NIEMEYER, H-G and H. SCHUBART *Toscanos. Die altpunische Faktorei an der Mündung des Río de Velez*. Madrider Forschungen Bd. 6.1, Berlin, 1969.

NIEMEYER, H-G and H. SCHUBART *Trayamar. Die phönizischen Kammergräber und die Niederlassung an der Algarrobo-Mündung*. Madrider Beiträge Bd. 4, Berlin, 1975.

NIEMEYER, H-G, ed., *Phönizier im Westen*.

Madrider Beiträge Bd. 8, Mainz-am-Rhein, 1982 [a finely published collection of important essays, all of them with original ideas].

OLMO LETE, G. del and M. E. AUBET, eds., *Los Fenicios en la Península Ibérica*. 2 vols., Barcelona, 1986 [chiefly essays on linguistic matters, but all well-written].

PELLICER CATALAN, M. *Excavaciones en la necropolis púnica 'Laurita' del Cerro de San Cristóbal, Almuñécar, Granada*, Excavaciones Arqueológicas en España vol. 17, Madrid, 1963.

RIPOLL PERELLO, E. and E. SANMARTI GREGO, eds., *Simposio Internacional de Colonizaciones, Barcelona-Ampurias, 1971*, Barcelona, 1974 [good collection of essays, especially those relating to Catalonia].

WHITTAKER, C. R. 'The Western Phoenicians: Colonisation and Assimilation', *Proceedings of the Cambridge Philological Society Nº 200*, 58–79, 1974 [important and stimulating study, with some inaccuracies that Niemeyer (1982) corrected].

## 4 The orientalizing period

Anon. *Primeras Jornadas Arqueológicas sobre Colonizaciones Orientales. Huelva Arqueologica VI*, 1982, Huelva, 1983 [the articles complement those in Niemeyer 1982; some are Spanish translations of German originals].

ALMAGRO GORBEA, M. *El Bronce Final y el Periódo Orientalizante en Extremadura*. Bibliotheca Praehistorica Hispana 14, Madrid, 1975 [an excellent book containing many photographs and a good essay on the orientalizing period].

AUBET, M. E. *La Necrópolis de Setefilla en Lora del Río (Sevilla) (Túmulo A)*, CSIC, Barcelona, 1975.

AUBET, M. E. *La Necrópolis de Setefilla (Túmulo B)*, CSIC, Barcelona, 1978.

AUBET, M. E. *Marfiles Fenicios del Bajo Guadalquivir, I. Cruz del Negro*, Studia Archaeologica, 52, Valladolid, 1979.

AUBET, M. E. *Marfiles Fenicios del Bajo Guadalquivir, II. Acebuchal y Alcantarilla*, Studia Archaeologica 63, Valladolid, 1980.

AUBET, M. E., M. R. SERNA, J. L. ESCACENA and M. M. RUIZ DELGADO *La Mesa de Setefilla: Lora del Río*

*(Sevilla)*, *Campaña de 1979*, Excavaciones Arqueológicas en España vol. 122, Madrid, 1983 [five excellent, meticulous studies by Professor Aubet].

GARRIDO ROIZ, J. P. and E. ORTA GARCIA *Excavaciones en la Necrópolis de 'La Joya', Huelva. II. Excavaciones Arqueológicas en España* vol. 96, Madrid, 1978.

KOCH, M. 1984 *Tarschisch und Hispanien*. Madrider Forschungen Bd. 14, Berlin, 1984 [linguistic study of the name 'Tarshish' and its variants].

MALUQUER DE MOTES, J. *Tartessos: La Ciudad sin Historia*, Barcelona, 1972.

MATA CARRIAZO, J. de *Tartessos y El Carambolo. Investigaciones Arqueológicas sobre la Protohistoria de la Baja Andalucia*, Madrid, 1973 [the prime description of the treasure of El Carambolo, and the results of excavations at the site. It has fine pictures, but a confused text, which cannot be taken literally].

## 5 The Greeks in the far west

Anon. *Colonización Griega y Mundo Indigena en la Península Ibérica, 8–9 Junio 1978 (Madrid)*. Symposium published in the *Archivo Español de Arqueologia* vol. 52, Nos. 139–40, 1979

ARRIBAS, A., Mª. G. TRIAS, D. CERDA and J. DE HOZ *El Barco de El Sec (Costa de Calviá, Mallorca)*, Mallorca, 1987.

BLAZQUEZ, J. M. *Tartessos y los Origenes de la Colonización Fenicia en Occidente*, (2nd ed.), Salamanca, 1975.

BOARDMAN, J. *The Greeks Overseas* (2nd ed.), London and New York, 1984.

CARPENTER, R. *Beyond the Pillars of Hercules*, London, 1973.

FERNANDEZ JURADO, J. *La Presencia Griega Arcaica en Huelva (2nd ed.)* Monografias Arqueológicas, Colección Excavaciones en Huelva 1/1984, Huelva, 1985.

FINLEY, M. I. *The Ancient Economy*, London, 1973.

GARCIA Y BELLIDO, A. *Hispania Graeca* (3 vols.), Barcelona, 1948 [the standard account of Greeks in Spain, with fine photographs; many of the objects and sites illustrated are lost, or now destroyed].

GUADAN, A. M. de *Las Monedas de Plata de Emporion y Rhode I*. Anales y Boletín de los Museos de Arte de Barcelona, Años 1955–1956, vol. XII, Barcelona, 1968.

PICAZO, M. *La Cerámica Atica de Ullastret*, Barcelona, 1977.

SANMARTI I GREGO, E. 'Las cerámicas de Barniz Negro y su función delimitadora de los horizontes Ibéricos Tardios' (siglos III–I a.C.), in *La Baja Epoca de la Cultura Ibérica*, Ed. Asociación Española de Amigos de Arqueologia, p. 163–79, Madrid, 1981 [a lucid account, especially important for the late Greek pottery production in Spain].

SHEFTON, B. 1982 'Greeks and Greek Imports in the South of the Iberian Peninsula. The Archaeological Remains', in Niemeyer 1982 (ed.) p. 337–70.

TRIAS, G. *Cér1amicas Griegas de la Península Ibérica* (2 vols.), Valencia, 1967 [this fine study is confined to *decorated* Greek pottery only. The introductory essay is still a model of its kind].

VILLARONGA, L. 1977 *The Aes Coinage of Emporion*, British Archaeological Reports Sup. Ser. 23, Oxford, 1977.

## 6 Carthaginian archaeology in Spain

ASTRUC, M. *La Necrópolis de Villaricos*. Informes y Memorias de al C.G.E.A. Nº 25, Madrid, 1951.

AUBET SEMMLER, M. E. *La Cueva d'es Cuyram, Ibiza*. Instituto de Arqueologia y Prehistoria, Universidad de Barcelona. Publicaciones Eventuales Nº 15, Barcelona, 1969.

GAMER-WALLERT, I. *Ägyptische und Ägyptisierende Funde von der Iberischen Halbinsel*. Bhft. z. Tübinger Atlas des vorderen Orients (Reihe B, Nº 21), Weisbaden, 1978.

GONZALEZ WAGNER, E. C. *Fenicios y Cartagineses en la Península Ibérica*. Doctoral Dissertation, Universidad Complutense de Madrid, published as Nº 30/83, Madrid, 1983.

GUERRERO AYUSO, V. M. *Indigenisme i Colonització Púnica a Mallorca*, Palma de Mallorca, 1985.

MOLINA FAJARDO, F., A. RUIZ HERNANDEZ and C. HUERTA JIMENEZ 1982. *Almuñécar en la antigüedad. La Necrópolis fenicio-púnica de Puente de Noy*, Granada, 1982.

TARRADELL, M. and M. FONT *Eivissa Cartaginesa*, Barcelona, 1975 [clear and authoritative account of Punic Ibiza].

WHITTAKER, C. R. Carthaginian Imperialism in the Fifth and Fourth Centuries, in P. D. A. GARNSEY and C. R. WHITTAKER, eds., *Imperialism in the Ancient World* p 59–90; apparatus 297–302 and 360–68, Cambridge, 1978.


## 7 The first towns

BATS, M. and H. TREZINY, eds., *Le Territoire de Marseille Grecque; Actes de la Table-rond d'Aix-en-Provence, 16 mars 1985*, Provence, 1986.

BURILLO MOZOTA, F. 1980 *El Valle Medio del Ebro en Epoca Ibérica*. Institución Fernándo El Católico CSIC, Pub. N° 751, Zaragoza, 1980.

ESCACENA, J. L. 'Gadir' in G. DEL OLMO LETE and M. E. AUBET, (eds., *Los Fenicios en la Península Ibérica II*, 39–58, Barcelona, 1985.

EUZENNAT, M. Ancient Marseille in the light of recent excavations. *American Journal of Archaeology 84*, 133–140, 1980.

FORTEA, J. and J. BERNIER *Recintos y Fortificaciónes Ibéricas en la Bética*. Memorias del Seminario de Prehistoria y Arqueología No. 2, Salamanca, 1970.

HODGES, R. *Dark Age Economics. The Origins of Towns and Trade* AD *600–1000*, Bristol, 1982.

ISSERLIN, B. S. J. 'Some common features in Phoenician/Punic town planning'. *Rivista di Studi Fenici 1*, 135–52, 1973.

MARTIN ORTEGA, M. A. 1985 *Ullastret. Poblat Ibèric* (English translation: *The Iberian Settlement at Ullastret*), Barcelona, 1985 (an excellent short guide to the town, with clear photographs; the only modern account of the excavations at Ullastret].

RUIZ DE ARBULO BAYONA, J. 'Emporion y Rhode. Dos asentamientos portuarios en el golfo de Rosas'. *Arqueología Espacial vol IV*, 115–140 (ed. F. BURILLO, Teruel), Teruel, 1984) [full references to Emporion included].

SCHELDERMANN, H. 'The idea of a town; typology, definitions and approaches to the study of the Medieval town in northern Europe', *World Archaeology 2*, 115–127, 1970.

SJOBERG, G. *The Pre-industrial City: Past and Present*, Glencoe, Illinois, 1960.


## 8 Art and the ideology of power

ALMAGRO GORBEA, M. 'El monumento de Alcoy. Aportación preliminar a la arquitectura funeraria ibérica'. *Trabajos de Prehistoria 39*, 161–210, 1982.

ALMAGRO GORBEA, M. 'Pozo Moro', *Madrider Mitteilungen 24*, 177–293, 1983 [a first-class account of Almagro's discoveries at Pozo Moro; full bibliography, and splendid photographs].

BLAZQUEZ, J. M. and J. GONZALEZ NAVARRETE 'The Phokaian Sculpture of Obulco in Southern Spain', *American Journal of Archaeology 89*, 61–69, plates 9–20, 1985.

CHAPA BRUNET, T. *La Escultura Ibérica Zoomorfa*. Madrid, 1985 [the best catalogue of stone sculptures to have been written for years, accompanied by good photographs].

CHAPA BRUNET, T. *Influjos Griegos en la Escultura Zoomorfa Ibérica*. Iberia Graeca. Ser. Arq. N° 2, CSIC, Madrid, 1986.


## 9 The new gods

BLAZQUEZ, J. M. *Religiones Preromanas: tomo II. Primitivas religiones ibéricas*, Madrid, 1983 [a remarkable survey of ancient cults and rites in Iberia, with abundant descriptions and pictures. Textual sources are more important than archaeological ones, and dominate the discussion].

GARCIA Y BELLIDO, A. 'Hercules Gaditanus', *Archivo Español de Arqueología 36*, 68–153, 1964.

NICOLINI, G. *Les bronzes figurés des sanctuaries ibériques*, Paris, 1969.

PADRO I PARCERISA, J. *Egyptian-Type Documents from the Mediterranean Littoral of the Iberian Peninsula Before the Roman Conquest. I Introductory Survey*, Leiden, 1980.

PADRO I PARCERISA, J. *Egyptian-Type Documents from the Mediterranean Littoral of the Iberian Peninsula before the Roman Conquest. III: Study of the Material: Andalusia*, Leiden, 1985.

PRESEDO VELO, F. J. *La Necrópolis de Baza*, Excavaciones Arqueológicas en España vol. 119, Madrid, 1982 [the discoverer's original account of the dig which brought the 'Dama de Baza' to light].

ROSSELLO-BORDOY, G., R. SANCHEZ-CUENCA and P. de MONTANER ALONSO 'Imhotep, hijo de Ptah'. *Mayurqa 13*, 123–142, Trabajos del Museo de Mallorca, 1974.

TSIRKIN, J. B. 'The labours, death and resurrection of Melquart as depicted on the gates of the Gades' Herakleion'. *Revista de Studi Fenici 9 (1)*, 21–27, 1981.

**Cancho Roano (Badajoz)**

BLANCO FREIJEIRO, A. 'Cancho Roano: Un monumento proto-histórico en los confines de la antigua Lusitanía', *Boletín de la Real Academía de Historia 178*, 225–41, 1981.

MALUQUER DE MOTES, J. *El Santuario de Zalamea de la Serena, Badajoz, 1978–81.* Universidad de Barcelona Instituto de Arqueología y Prehistoria vol. IV, Barcelona, 1981.

MALUQUER DE MOTES, J. *El Santuario protohistórico de Zalamea de la Serena, Badajoz. II.* 1981–1982. Univ. de Barcelona, Inst. de Arqu. y Prehist. vol. V, Barcelona, 1983.

MALUQUER DE MOTES, J., S. CELESTINO, F. GRACIA and G. MUNILLA *El Santuario Protohistórico de Zalamea de la Serena, Badajoz. III, 1983–1986.* Univ. de Barcelona, Inst. de Arqu. y Prehist. vol. XIV, Barcelona, 1986 [all of these works on the great building at Cancho Roano are hurried and incomplete, but they are the discoverers' original accounts. Details are contradictory, descriptions partial, but the splendour of the finds is obvious].

**10 Writing and the uses of literacy**

ALVES DIAS, M. M. and L. COELHO 'Notável lápide protohistórica da herdade da Abóbada-Almodôvar'. *O Arqueólogo Portugues, Ser. III (5)*, 181–190, 1971.

HARRIS R. *The Origin of Writing*, London, 1986.

DE HOZ, J. 'Escritura e influencia clásica en los pueblos preromanos de la Península'. *Archivo Español de Arqueología 52*, 227–250, 1979.

MALUQUER DE MOTES, J. *Epigrafía Prelatina de la Península Ibérica*, Barcelona, 1968 [probably the most complete catalogue readily available of ancient Iberian inscriptions and their transliterations].

NAVEH, J. *Early History of the Alphabet*, Jerusalem, 1982.

SOLIER, Y. 'Découverte d'inscriptions sur plombs en écriture ibérique dans un entrepôt de Pech Maho (Sijean)'. *Revue Archéologique de Narbonnaise (Montpellier) 12*, 55–123, 1979.

**11 Fruits of the earth: mining, farming and manufacturing**

CUADRADO, E. 'Tumbas principescas de el Cigarralejo.' *Madrider Mitteilungen 9*, 148–186, 1968.

PERICOT, L. *Cerámica Ibérica*, Barcelona, 1977 [full of colour photographs, accompanied by a decent text].

PLA BALLESTER, E. 'Instrumentos de trabajo ibéricos en la región valenciana', in M. TARRADELL, ed., *Estudios de Economía Antigua de la Península Ibérica*, 143–190, Barcelona, 1968.

RADDATZ, K. *Die Schatzfunde der Iberischen Halbinsel.* Madrider Forschungen Bd. 5, Berlin, 1969.

ROTHENBERG, B. and A. BLANCO FREIJEIRO *Ancient Mining and Metallurgy in South-West Spain*, London, 1981.

ROTHENBERG, B. and F. GRACIA PALOMERO 'The Río Tinto Enigma – no more', *Institute for Archaeo-Metallurgical Studies: Newsletter No. 8*, 3–5, London, 1986.

**Epilogue**

Anon. *La Baja Epoca de la Cultura Ibérica.* Actas de la Mesa Redonda Celebrada en Conmemoración del Decimo Aniversario de la Asociación Española de Amigos de Arqueología. Madrid-Marzo 1979, Madrid, 1981.

# List of illustrations

The author and publishers are indebted to the persons and institutions who have granted permission to reproduce photographs and illustrations. Unless otherwise credited, photographs were provided by the Instituto Arqueológico Alemán, Madrid, through the kindness of Herr P. Witte and Dr Hermanfrid Schubart. GO indicates drawings after J. P. Garrido Roiz and E. Orta García, *Excavaciones en la Necrópolis de 'La Joya', Huelva. II. Excavaciones Arqueológicas en España*, vol. 96, Madrid, 1978. MM indicates drawings after J. Maluquer De Motes, *Epigrafía Prelatina de la Península Ibérica*, Barcelona, 1968. 'Niemeyer' refers to H-G Niemeyer *Phönizier im Westen*, Madrider Beiträge Bd. 8, Mainz-am-Rhein, 1982. Maps unless otherwise credited were provided by the author.

*Title page*: Iberian stone carving: 'Dama de Elche' from Elche (Alicante).

1 Map of the Mediterranean indicating Phoenician and Greek sites.
2 Map showing extent of Iberian culture.
3 Map of Iberian peninsula pinpointing major sites.
4 Tartessian bronze jug from Don Benito (Badjoz).
5 Map indicating geographical regions, rivers and modern towns.
6 (*Top*) Map indicating Iberian topography. (*Bottom*) Map indicating areas of wet and dry climate in Iberia.
7 Map locating various Bronze Age cultural groups.
8 Map locating major groups of Bronze Age pottery.
9 Map indicating locations of grave stelas.
10 Grave stela from southern Portugal.
11 Stela from warrior's grave from Solana de Cabañas (Logrosán, Cáceres). Photo Museo Arqueológico Nacional, Madrid.
   Stela from Luna (Zaragoza).

Photo Ma. Luisa de Sus, Museo Arqueológico, Zaragoza.
13 Examples of weapons from Bronze Age Spain.
14 Gold collar from Sintra. Reproduced by kind permission of the Trustees of the British Museum, London.
15 Gold jugs and bracelets from the Villena hoard.
16 Gold bowls and bracelets from the Villena hoard.
17 Ground plan of a Bronze Age excavated village. Modified after A. Beltrán Martínez 'Las casas del poblado de la I Edad del Hierro del Cabezo de Monleón (Caspe)', *Boletín del Museo de Zaragoza N°. 3*, Zaragoza, 1984.
18 Map of Almuñécar. After A. García y Bellido *Fenicios y Cartagineses en Occidente*, Madrid, 1942, fig. 3.
19 View from Toscanos, looking towards the Mediterranean.
20 Chronology of main settlements and cemeteries of the western Phoenicians in southern Spain. After H. Schubart, 'Asentamientos fenicios en la costa meridional de la península Ibérica', in *Primeras Jornadas Arqueológicas sobre Colonizaciones Orientales. Huelva Arqueológica VI*, (anon.), 1983, pp. 71–100, fig. 17.
21 View of four tombs cut into the hillside at Villaricos.
22 Interior of Tomb 37 at Trayamar (Malaga).
23 Phoenician bronze incense burner found at Almayate Bajo, Cerro de la Peñón (Malaga).
24 Phoenician bronze deer found in Spain. Reproduced by kind permission of the Trustees of the British Museum, London.
25 Two bronze statuettes of Phoenician manufacture.
26 Map locating Phoenician colonies in southern Spain; also important Tartessian sites. After M. E. Aubet, 'Zur Problematik des

169

97    Transcription from three stelas of the southwest. After MM: 145.

98    Letter with three messages in Levantine Iberian script. After MM: 132–34.

99    Letters of the Levantine Iberian alphabet.

100   Letter written on lead in Levantine Iberian alphabet. After MM: 130–31.

101   Pottery bearing a Levantine Iberian inscription. After MM: 118–19.

102   Plan of ore lodes and archaeological sites at Río Tinto mines. After B. Rothenberg and A. Blanço Freijeiro *Ancient Mining and Metallurgy in South-West Spain*, London, 1981, fig. 108.

103   Schematic section of Río Tinto showing silver ore lodes. After B. Rothenberg and F. Gracia Palomero 'The Rio Tinto Enigma – no more', *Institute for Archaeo-Metallurgical Studies Newsletter No. 8*, London, 1986.

104   View of Corta Lago. Photo Professor B. Rothenberg, London.

105   View of the Cerro Colorado (Río Tinto, Huelva). Photo Professor B. Rothenberg, London.

106,  Wrought-iron tools. Based on
107   illustrations in E. Plá Ballester 'Instrumentos de trabajo ibéricos en la región valenciana', in M. Tarradell, ed., *Estudios de Economía Antigua de la Península Ibérica*, Barcelona, 1968.

108   Shapes of Iberian pottery made between 500 and 200 BC. After A. García y Bellido, *Arte Ibérico en España*, Madrid, 1980, figs. 131–2.

109   *Kalathos* (hat-shaped pot) decorated with bird of prey.

110   Detail of a beast from a painted Iberian pot.

111   Detail of a scene from an Iberian *pithos*.

112   'Warrior vase' from Iberian town of Liria (Valencia).

# Index